A LIVING TESTIMONY

WHO WILL CRY FOR ME?

SHERREE

Outskirts Press, Inc.
Denver, Colorado

Contents

Who Will Cry for Me?

My real life story of trials, tribulations, abuse and drama

My story is probably one that hundreds if not thousands can identify with. Read, and hopefully overcome obstacles in your lives.

This is not a book about pity or getting revenge on anyone, instead it's about the continuation of getting *over* everything and everyone who abused or hurt me and hopefully, by the grace of God, this book will help others to get past their abuses, trials, tribulations and drama.

Sherree

Acknowledgements

THROUGH it all Jesus carried me and showed me time after time that He would sustain and keep me. I thank God for His mercy and grace for bringing me through each and every trial when I thought and sometimes even wanted to die. Thank you Lord for making this book possible.

To my husband Clarence, with special thanks for all of your love and support. For all the hours and years that we have talked, prayed, laughed, cried, and loved, it has all been worth it. No matter what my goals have been, you've shown me that you have been my #1 supporter and my rock. Thank you for always having my back. I could not have completed this project without you, thank you my soul mate, my love.

Thanks to my birthday son Leon who said "that's tough, I'm proud of you mom", that meant the world to me. I know that I can call on you anytime, and you've always been there for me. To Janain, the son that always has the ability to make me laugh, even when I've wanted to cry. You are an encouragement to me, thank you son. To my son LaTyre' who is the "apple of my eye." You don't know how much you all mean to me.

To the rest of my family, friends and colleagues who have shown your love for me through the years and even for those of you that have shown me the opposite, it is you who also helped to make this endeavor possible, for without you, my life story would have been impossible. Thank you all.

To my girl Pamela Steplight, thank you for being such an encourager. It is nice to have a friend who is steady, easy; quiet yet is strong and gives you just the right amount of encouragement when you need it most. You are all that. Thank you sister girl for all of your help, advice, and support and for always having the time just for me.

To my friend and co-laborer in the Ministry, Sister Sadie McGregor, you have helped to push me through this home stretch with your warm encouragement and just by saying "I have faith in you," those words helped me to finish the fire that was set forth. Thank you my friend.

To my friend Vandana Prasad, thank you for being constant, consistent and genuine. You are the real deal.

Introduction

"It was during those times that I carried you."

It would be nice if I could say that I came from a family of a natural mother and a father full of love, family outings, and summer vacations. A family who is kind to each other, sharing moments of "just because" talks, where the siblings all get along and ultimately grow up to become successful men and women who still get along and are there for each other. And yes, it would be wonderful if my mom could have been a loving stay at home mom, or maybe even working outside the home part-time and volunteering at my school or going on a field trip with me and my class once in a while. But the reality is that I did not have a family like this, as probably so many thousands, if not millions of people didn't. It's so ironic that the very first prayer that was taught to me was "now I lay me down to sleep, I pray the Lord my soul to keep, if I should die before I wake, I pray the Lord my soul to take." I was a child who *did* want to die rather than to keep living getting gagged, bound and beaten. ...I'm not sure just who taught me that prayer but I am almost positive it was one of the close abusers. The reason I say close is because, among others, there were a couple of them living right under the same roof as myself. Here is my story.

Mary Ana,
is the oldest of us. She left Mississippi in 1968 and although she has been back once, she just has not been back there to live since. The first time I spoke with her was by phone in the mid 1980's. Since I was taken from Mississippi, at almost three years old, we did not meet in person again until 2001 when I went to Phoenix to visit her, I was forty five years old. She is the mother of nine children and has been constantly, consistently and continuously involved in their lives. I commend her.

Neal,
is the second oldest. He has one daughter who lives in Phoenix. She was raised in Phoenix, that is where her mother lived. When I went to Phoenix in 2001 I got a chance to meet my niece, her husband their sons and her mother. What a beautiful young woman (as is the case with all of my nieces.) Everyone says that this particular niece looks just like me.

Wendell,

is the third oldest and is the father of five children. He has been closer to me over the years than any of my siblings, even when we argue. We often have talks about how we all grew up and how our mother broke the bonds between us. Even though Wendell and I don't see a lot of each other, we have always tried to make it a point to stay connected with each other by phone. When Mother passed away in 2003, Wendell was the only one of my siblings to meet my husband and all of my children when he came to Portland. I will always be grateful to him for that.

Audra,

is the fourth oldest and she is like the Continental divide, directly in the middle. There are three of us younger than she and three older. Audra is somewhat a woman of few words. But I'm sure she has had more than her share of trials and troubles. Audra is the only one of us who has not married nor has children.

Lutricia,

is the third youngest and tries to act like the oldest. She is the one who was with me when I was given away to go to Portland. Lutricia has told me in the past that we were holding on to each other and crying for me not to be taken. She would have been about six years old at that time. I believe my sister loves to be in control of all situations, she has a heart of gold but has an underlying need to always have the upper hand. I know she and Audra has experienced their own tremendous struggles and if they would, could share their own stories.

Marlena,

has experienced childbirth four times, two marriages, one bad, one good, survived a nervous breakdown, being sexually abused as a child, by grown men but through it all, still managed to survive. Has been disregarded by children that was either raised or helped raised by her, and quite often even experienced abuse by having toxic "friends". I believe that when you stack weight upon itself, the bottom of the pile bears the most weight. It carries the most burdens. This weight that I am talking about is the fact that I believe all of us have at least a little bit of dysfunction but the last three of us carry something extra that in my mind the others' don't. That may be (1) an extra keenness of other's spirit and soul, (2) a strong will that does not tolerate any signs of weakness, humbleness, or humility at any cost and if any of those are detected, your person will get trampled on with no mercy or remorse. (3) Last but certainly not least, a will that is tolerable of others, but yet unemotional, lives her own life, but unattached, can love, but won't let other's in on it. As I have gotten to know my siblings over the years, I realize that I still do not really *know* them and they do not know me. To sum it up, ultimately, the bond is missing.

Penny,

my youngest sister was not born yet when I was taken. The first time I met her was around 1968. I was fourteen she was about eleven or twelve. Penny is very outspoken, which, I would have to say, most of us are, but each in a different way. She has one daughter and I would say Penny still likes to get her party on.

The Two Mothers – Layla

I don't know a lot about my biological mother, but I do know that she was generally soft spoken, and in my eyes, probably not too self confident. Born into poverty in the Delta of Mississippi, Layla, from what I have gathered over the years from older siblings, did not have a normal teenage life. I'm told she was one of five children including a twin brother who was killed later while he was crossing the street. Layla was a reasonably attractive young woman with a low key demeanor. Over the years, I initiated phone calls to her, but never received any from her. I will never know the answer to the question of why she did not initiate any calls to me. My earliest remembrance of her is when I met her at age fourteen, which is the first time I went back to Mississippi after being taken away. She and three of my sisters all came to the airport to see me. It was a little awkward for me, but it was a lasting memory of my biological mother and my sisters. All of my sisters and brothers say that I am the striking image of our mother. Even our mannerism is similar. I can see that. No one really knows why she gave all but one of us away. She kept my youngest sister, Penny. My thoughts are that it probably was because of who our fathers were and the shame of it all. To my knowledge, Penny is the only one of us who has a different father. Lucky her. Layla was a victim herself of severe molestation. It has never been discussed by her to me who my biological father is. Rumors were going around about it when I was a young teenager, but to me they were nothing more than that, just rumors. Layla had her first child at about fourteen years old. She has a sister who has just as many children as Layla does, about the same ages as me and my siblings are.

According to my sister, Mary Ana, who is about twelve years older than me, she remembers hearing sounds coming from Layla's room. This man had to be mentally sick. He was molesting Layla while her daughter was in the other room. God only knows how many times at that point she had been molested. I'm told he used to have her go fishing with him and was probably molesting her there too, along with her sister Carmen. It goes deeper than that. This man, this molester, Azell Arthur Sr, the man I'm told fathered me, had a son and a daughter by his wife, my grandmother, Lottie, but he was not Layla's father. Starting to get the picture? Layla was repeatedly being molested by her stepfather who also fathered me and five of my siblings while he was married to my grandmother. This sort of thing was prevalent down south, especially in the back woods. No one knows why Layla had so many children by him. She was twenty three years old when I was born. I was the last child born to this man and Layla, but not her last child. I often wondered what my grandmother thought about all of this. How could she have sat by and allowed it to happen? While her education level may have been slightly low, no one really knows what she thought or how she took all of this. Was she subservient to him? Was she afraid? Did she have self esteem issues? Why would someone allow this type of behavior to go on? It appears that she just accepted the fact that her husband wanted her daughter. It is not clear to me, but when that man died, he died with me never knowing nor seeing him. I'm sure at one point in my life, with my hot temper, there would have been a select choice of words I would have had to say to him. It is not known to me if Layla's biological father, my grandfather, knew that his daughter's stepfather was raping her and fathering her children. The curse of abuse seemed to have picked back up with me when Layla made the decision to give me to Mother and let her take me to Portland. It seemed that when the molestation ended for her, it began again with me at the age of six. All have since passed on now, but left so many unanswered questions behind. I don't know when the others passed, but I do know that Layla took all of her answers to my questions with her to the grave on September 5, 2002.

Mother/Robbie

Mother has said that almost immediately I started calling her "Mother". It seems so hard to believe that a small child could just suddenly start calling a stranger "Mother." But hard to believe as it may be, apparently I did and I don't remember calling her anything else. Apparently it was not a struggle for me to start leaning on someone who was not my mother. Mother didn't have any natural children. I have said many times in my adult life that if a woman cannot or does not have children, God has a specific reason to have allowed this. *We* may not know why, but there is a reason.

1

Broken Bonds

DURING one of our brief conversations, Layla has told me that I was born in 1955, in the early morning hour of about five am, in the Delta of Mississippi. The little town was called Tribbetts, Washington County. I'm sure it was cold because it was February. The Delta of Mississippi is a place that holds a very proud but impoverished people because of the spirit of the bondage of slavery and the remnants of poverty and hardships leftover from slavery itself. Two thirds of the Delta was Black and because of the extended low price of cotton, a large number had gone deeply into debt, therefore being forced to sell off their land between 1910 and 1920. My grandmother would have been in that number. When she had children, there was very little or no work except farming, or I should say "tenant farming" and sharecropping.

My biological mother, Layla, was born into a time

of extreme poverty, hardships, and the cruelness that life itself can bring; I have grown to believe that she had no way out. She may have given up at a very early age, only God knows now. She would apparently suffer from the time she was born until the time she died, what with extreme poverty looming everywhere, a man constantly, consistently and precisely molesting her for years giving her baby after baby, and living with what has got to be more shame than one woman can handle alone. My prayer is that she is now resting.

They named me Marlena. It seems that I was even born into confusion. There must have been some discrepancy about what last name to use because on my birth certificate it shows the last name of Arthur, which is the last name of the man who fathered me, but the rest of my siblings have the last name of Cantrell, which is my mother's maiden name.

I am the sixth child of five girls and two boys. My biological mother, Layla, later moved us from the Delta to Clinton. My biological father is unknown to me although I do know his name and have heard some things about him, but no first hand knowledge. Knowing what I know now, it's probably better that he is unknown to me. Most, if not all, of my siblings do know at least who he is and have seen him. They know more about him than I do. I'm not even sure when he died. It's been told to me he passed in the 1950's right after I was born. Then it was told to me later he passed away in the 1970's. So apparently, it is not known for sure when Azell Arthur passed away.

It has been difficult in my lifetime to try and piece together what really happened and why our mother chose to give her children away, seemingly so easy to various families, some of which she hardly knew. Some of my siblings have never talked to me about their childhood and how they felt about this whole situation. My eldest sister would prefer to not talk about it (but we have) and she says that it is in the past, we are all grown and survived it. I agree with her to an extent but I believe some things need to be told so that light can be shed upon them and notes can be compared then continued healing can take place. I'm sure that each one of us probably could have used good spiritual counseling at some point in our lives. Each of us was torn in some kind of way, in my opinion by the direct actions of our birth mother.

One of my brothers told me that he grew up in a very good and loving home where he was taught and shown love, with a fairly good life, but that every time our mother would come to see him (which, according to him was not very often,) he would always ask her when she was going to get him back and she always told him that she would come back and get him, but that day never came. I'm sure that tore his heart when he would realize that his mother was not coming back and after so long, he would realize that it turned out to be an untruth.

Another one of my siblings has told me that she had a very abusive childhood. I'm not quite sure how she was abused because we have never gone into detail about it and I have not asked her, but I know it probably still runs through her mind and her spirit just like it does mine. It's up to us what we do with it when we find ourselves thinking on it. I chose to try and mask it with alcohol early in life. For about five years during my early twenties alcohol was my way to escape, so to speak. I am so thankful that God made me look at myself and woke me up before something really, really bad happened to me.

Bearing the brunt and being the product of several different kinds of abuse, there is no way that words can express the feeling and impact that each and every one of these acts had on my person. These eight types of abuse, abandonment, physical, sexual, emotional, mental, psychological, verbal, and later, my own domestic violence would unfortunately be the tools that would be the building blocks of my character, but they do not define me as a person or as a woman.

It is understandable how some people escape into multiple personalities caused by emotional trauma. It is something that one probably never really gets over but you learn to deal with it by talking about it. Talking it out helps to promote healing and healing promotes forgiveness. Hiding it will not make it go away. Writing about it, helps if it hurts too much to talk about it. One can channel it away from themselves by doing something positive for others. For me, doing all of those things has helped.

The first abuse that I experienced was that my birth mother gave me and five of my siblings to various people, not realizing, or perhaps just not caring, what kind of home she was putting us into. Abandonment is such a cruel and ugly thing to do to any child. I'm sure this is definitely a place where rejection started to impact my life and distrust started to develop in me towards people and perhaps more so with my own female gender. To abandon something or someone means to leave completely and finally, to forsake utterly. That, I would say is exactly what Layla did.

To my knowledge there was never any remorse or phone calls to keep in touch over the years. In fact, it seemed quite the opposite, probably not even realizing that she would be the cause of breaking every kind of bond that a human could have. The bonds that help to mold a child throughout its life: Mother/daughter bond, brother/sister, sister/sister and just general relational bonds.

I don't remember how I felt as such a very young child when my birth mother made the decision to give me to her first cousin, Robbie, who I would grow to call Mother. I'm not sure if it would have made any difference if I had said "no" when Mother asked me if I wanted to go to Portland with her. I probably thought that was what I was supposed to say.

I came to the conclusion later in life that the Mother who *raised* me had very severe anger problems. She was the physical and verbal abuser, all through my tender years (through age fifteen). She discouraged me, told me I was nothing, and that I would never be anything. There were years of stripping and robbing my inner being of itself and self-worth, along with extreme harsh, over the edge beatings. Being tied up and gagged while getting beat, for me was the worst. No one even knew this type of abuse was going on. The list goes on to include the stepbrother who was the first to molest me at five years old, as well as others.

The domestic violence that I would experience later in life as well as the nervous breakdown that I suffered was nothing compared to all the years of my childhood abuse and atrocities. I was grown up, could and did walk away from the domestic violence, but as a child I knew nothing about running or walking away. I had nowhere to turn and no where to go. God has truly brought me from a mighty long way.

It is my intention to graphically tell my story in this book to encourage and to help others to heal, as well as to continue to promote my own inner healing. I know that things do happen for a reason that is no secret. But do we, or perhaps the better question is, *can* we always figure out what the reason is that bad things happen to innocent people? Or why good things happen to bad people? I do know that our thoughts are not God's thoughts, but I can tell you this, that in the beginning He made this world perfect, but it became imperfect, and in an imperfect world, people need people. If I have never gone through anything, or if you have never gone through anything, how can you help anyone? I know that God was in the midst of my every cry. Every whip that was struck on my naked body was known to Him. Every molestation and violation of my tiny frame was seen by Him, and every attack of verbal abuse by mother telling me that I was nothing and that I would never be anything was heard by Him. How many more people have had these same things happen to them? This is where those of us who survived it all by the grace of God come in to say "I know exactly how you feel."

It's true I, myself did not come out smelling like a rose. There are still issues in my life. Remember, I said earlier that each one of us could probably have benefitted from some good Christian counseling? Well I definitely was not excluding myself. It is a known fact by those very close to me that I do not like to be crowded, so to speak. It has been a hard lesson to learn not to get too close to or allow others to get too close to me. I do like people, but at this stage in my life, because of all the garbage, stress, lies, cruelty of others and just out right selfish attitudes of people, shying away has become very easy. Meaning, I have to really work at not shutting people out, especially if I feel they are shutting me out. It feels like abandonment, rejection, and all those bad feelings all over again that was felt when I was a child. Ultimately, under what appears to be a hard shell is a very caring, sensitive person and that little girl is still deep down inside my soul.

By the time I was thirty three, my fourth and last child was born, this marked a turning point in my life. I believe that in everyone's life there is an event or something happens that *becomes* a turning point in one's life and for me, Jesus Christ was it. Learning how to really forgive was starting to take place.

Thank God for this turning point. The once fiery temper was *starting* to taper down. I am now in the winter stages of my life, saved and have the love of God in my heart. I have forgiven, but all the trauma that was viciously forced upon me so young for so many years, still lingers on. I accepted the Lord Jesus Christ in my heart, and it was the best decision I could have ever made.

No road is ever always just straight, there will always be a bend or turn within it

2

South to West

AT two and a half years old, a small child has no say in his or her decisions on their own lives as far as who they want to stay with. Mother asked me "do you want to go far away on the choo choo train?" Then according to her, I said "yes". She says she asked me "do you want to be my little girl" and again I said yes. Of course I don't remember any of this conversation. So right there bonds were being severed and broken when I was taken from Clinton, Mississippi to Portland, Oregon.

I can only imagine the trauma that my sister Lutricia and I were probably feeling as small children being ripped apart. Lutricia was most likely feeling it more because she was almost six and understood better than me. I often wonder if the two women ever even thought about the trauma and stress that this break-up of the last two children born at that time would cause? Probably not. This reminds me of what slavery must have felt like when the families were torn apart and forced to go to other slave owners.

It's not known how my other sisters and brothers handled being given away emotionally, but I am almost certain that anytime a baby or a small child is uprooted from their familiar surroundings, from the rest of their siblings and from the natural mother, dangerous consequences can occur for all involved. I believe that if not right then but later in life, my biological mother may have been traumatized to a degree by her own actions earlier in her life. A kind of delayed emotional reaction. I believe that each one of us, her children, was emotionally tainted by her actions of giving us away.

Mother, as I grew to call her, was a very strong-willed and somewhat hardened woman who believed that children should be perfect. Always minding their parents, never getting dirty, never getting the hair messed up and by no means never, ever get anything lower that a "C" on your report card. If any of these things happened I knew a lynching was going to occur. Looking back I realize how health, social and economic conditions can play a major role in one's life and well being. I understand more now why Mother got so over the edge angry. She had a serious anger problem coupled with hypertension (she was diagnosed eventually with this disease and was prescribed high blood pressure medication). The hypertension was compounded by economic instability. Mother's desire for a perfect family and a good life was about to come crashing down…big time.

It was 1957; I have seen pictures of me, Colin Sr and Colin Jr, at Christmas time. It is a cute picture but the face on the little girl is not happy. The little girl is probably having thoughts of her mother and the place she has been taken from, because in the picture she is looking up as if to say, 'I want to go home' the place where she was used to being all of her two and a half years of being on earth.

I remember Colin Sr as being good natured except when he and Mother fought. He smoked a pipe. Not a dope pipe like people smoke out of nowadays, but a real old fashioned pipe that burned tobacco. I liked smelling the strong aroma of the burning tobacco. Colin Sr was a short man who had a friendly face but he could have a strict demeanor when necessary. He always showed love towards me and treated me like his little girl. Colin Sr sometimes even called me "Little Gal". I always hated it when he'd call me Marlena May, which was my actual name. I don't really know what the root of he and Mother's problems were, but they seemed to argue and fight all the time, which ultimately ended up in a divorce. I think that if they could have made it, he would have been the only dad that I probably would have known.

In every picture of me as a small child however, I am never smiling in it. One of the first traumatic experiences that I remember probably around age four, was an ordeal in the bathtub, where mother was supposed to be washing my hair but for some reason she turned my head up and was letting water run up my nose instead of having me hold my head down to rinse it, she forced me to hold my head backwards with my face upwards to rinse my hair but attempting to drown me. I think by this time she was just angry at everything. She realized having a small child around was a lot of work and apparently had not thought this thing of getting an extra child through thoroughly enough. She already had Colin Jr, her stepson, but she wanted a complete set. The boy and the girl. Colin Sr on the other hand loved me. There was always drama and trauma around the house, especially any time I wet the bed, that was an automatic beating, (as I said before, she wanted a perfect child). Bedwetting was one of the things that I used to get beat a lot for.

It really was embarrassing to me because Mother would tell everyone that I wet in the bed and that I was just too lazy to get up. When I grew up and had children of my own, at least one of them wet the bed occasionally. I never believed in spanking them for bedwetting. It just did not seem right or logical that someone would get pleasure out of wetting in the bed intentionally, especially in the winter time when it was cold, rainy or snowy outside, and lay in a cold wet bed. She really was sadly mistaken in saying that I was just too lazy to get up and go to the bathroom. That was not the case. The bedwetting was not only at night but I would sometimes wet on myself in the daytime as well, if we were out somewhere. I remember very well why I'd wet on myself in the daytime, it was fear of Mother. Fear of what she would do if I said that I had to go to the bathroom. The fear of her humiliating me in public by saying very loudly, "I just asked you did you want to go to the bathroom and you said no." Well, I had said that I didn't need to go but if I had said yes I do need to go, she'd get mad and say, "we just left home, why didn't you use it before you left?" I was not a wild rambunctious child, so I always felt that the humiliation was undeserving, especially in public. I lived in a constant state of fear and embarrassment, which in itself, could wear on the mental state of any child. She finally took me to a doctor some years later, and there she discovered that I was not just "too lazy" to get up at night and go to the bathroom, that I indeed did have a problem. One thing that she found out was that I was a very sound sleeper almost like a dead person. This extremely sound sleep that I was experiencing may have been my way of inverting or getting lost in another world, in essence, my way of escaping into the unknown so much so that I *could* not wake up even to go to the bathroom. The other thing she discovered was that my tubing was very weak therefore I could not hold my water like most people could. Mother also found out that my plumbing was not emptying properly, which a surgery took place to correct it. I even remember the doctor telling her that it could be a nervous condition as well. Imagine that, a nervous condition, do you think?

Mother always believed that if she was going to beat me that I'd better not run, and I'd better not try to protect myself. To make sure of that, most of the time she would make me completely strip down and then tie me to my bed (both feet to the bed posts) and gag my mouth then beat until she got tired or until my skin was opened and bloodied from the extension cord, belt or switch (depending on how severe she wanted the beating to be). She gagged me so that the neighbors could not hear me screaming from the intense pain, and it would be stuffed so hard that my mouth inside and out would be broken and sore. My hands were also tied in front of me to insure that I would not be able to grab the switch or extension cord so that she could beat freely. I still cringe when I think of the countless times my fragile, beaten body would ooze with fresh blood from the lashes of an extension cord. Sometimes she would use three or four switches braided together (to make sure they would not break) and wale away on my skinny naked body.

I don't know why she took her anger out on me, or if she blamed me for the breakup with her husband, but she added to the trauma that had already taken place in my small but fragile life. One time she even hung me on a door, out of anger, probably for eating something without asking, I really don't remember. She hung me up on a door naked, and beat me. I still remember dangling there until she finally let me down. She was big on telling me to ask for any and everything in the kitchen. Never did I feel free in my home growing up. It seemed like she wanted me dead. I could not believe even as a child that this was always happening to me. Why else would these punishments be so cruel and unusual for a four, five or six year old?

The suffering began when I was very little and continued well into my teens. It was only by the grace of God that Mother did not kill me. It sounds preposterous to say that about someone who took me out of the sweltering heat of injustice and a level of poverty that no one on God's earth should ever have to be subjected to, but it is a very harsh reality for me. It hurts me still when I think about the aloneness of not having my siblings around me or anyone else for that matter whom I trusted. I remember how every time I got into trouble for something Mother always threatened to take me back to Mississippi and brutally remind me that my natural mother did not want me. But other times, especially when she had been drinking, she would say how she always wanted a boy and a girl and that's why she got me.

I remember once wanting to take violin lessons and Mother had already told me that I couldn't take the lessons, that she could not afford them. But to my ignorance, I allowed my third grade teacher to influence me by saying "maybe if you take it (the violin) home and let your mother see it, she'll change her mind." Big mistake, I was in for one of the worse beatings of my life. Because of my disobedience of bringing the violin home, when Mother walked in and seen the instrument placed very neatly on a rug in the middle of the floor she not only went off, she blew up. She started yelling and hollering at me. She locked my head between her knees exposing only my naked behind and away she beat with an extension cord. She told me I was nothing and that I would never be anything then spit in my face. I remember feeling so wounded, alone, scared and physically hurting. It is not clear what happened the rest of that evening but needless to say the violin went back to school the next day.

School was not so kind as well. I experienced racism by white kids and racism by some black kids as well when we moved to the other side of town. The other side of town, being Northeast Portland, was more of a mixture of nationalities but a lot more black families. Looking back, I now realize why I got picked on so much. I talked different and looked funny with pimples and blue-framed glasses with sandy hair. It never occurred to me why until just recently while watching a movie called "Lean on Me". There was a scene in that movie where a group of students was beating, harassing and ripping the clothes off of another student. I had seen that movie probably ten times or more over the years but it never occurred to me until my youngest son pointed out that they were picking on the "light skinned" girl.

Picking on the light skinned girl, what an awakening thought. That statement immediately took me back to the fifth and sixth grade. That is exactly what was happening to *me*. As I thought more and more and remembered all the boys and girls that would attack and gang up on me during those two horrible years at the grade school that I had to attend, not one of them was the same complexion as me. It got so bad, my parents had to finally take me out of that school and enroll me into a Catholic school for my seventh and eighth grade years.

There, it was more calm and less violent. It was a mixture of races and cultures. I felt much better there and made quite a few friends. However, by now my complex about the pimples was in full effect, but now also the harsh reality of my "light skin" had taken on a growing complex of it's own. Too light for most on one side, and too dark for the other side. As a result, things would quite often seem that no matter what I did, it was never enough or never good enough.

It boiled down to acceptance. It took some time to realize children are just like adults only in a smaller package. If they like you, they accept you for who are. If they don't like you, they find a way to make your life miserable. Adults should know how to communicate with each other and try to get to know one another instead of just going by hear say, or making their own negative assumptions about you, or holding something negative against you and not accepting you because you're not with the "in crowd", or even just because your beliefs are different. If I am willing to accept you with all of your imperfections, why can't you accept me with all of mine? I think it goes back to the simple basic biblical rule, "do unto others' as you want them to do unto you." If we all could just do that we might actually find out that the next person is truly a remarkable person.

I learned also that we as black people are just as color conscious as our white counterparts. We always want to know "is he or she white or black?" Or how light or dark is he or she? After giving birth to my third child, I was talking on the phone with one of my sisters, and she even asked me if my baby was light or dark. That immediately angered me, I asked her what difference did it make? She said "it doesn't make a difference I just wanted to know."

Growing up, listening to television and radio was one of my favorite things to do. It made me more and more interested in reading and writing. Mother, to my surprise always had Jet magazines around. I never really saw her read them, but she always had them around. So I started looking into them and liked reading them. The magazines, more than probably any single thing that I can think of, introduced me to a very positive side of my blackness and helped to teach me more about black awareness and black people who were not only role models, but also leaders and innovators. Reading and learning was a great pastime for me. In my young life there was not a lot of friends around, therefore, watching the news, listening to music, reading and writing became my interests. But I'm really thankful for Jet the magazines because it got me interested at a young age in knowing that my black people contributed to the past, present and the future of this society probably more so than my white counterparts, or at least a lot more than we are given credit for. I grew particularly interested in reading about the struggles in the lives of people that I knew from television like Muhammed Ali, Dr Martin Luther King, Dianne Carroll and others. The people in the magazines always looked good. It made me realize that just because you're going through some struggles, doesn't mean you have to look or act like you are. It prompted me to want to always look my best even when I've been at my absolute worst and that is a philosophy that has continued to stay with me from that day to this day. The models in the swimsuit also sparked my interest some years later for beauty. I recall that while Mother and I were in a grocery store, one day, not far from where we lived, I was approached by one of the local radio station disc jockeys to enter the local beauty pageant which was called Miss Tan. I knew about the pageant, it was held every year for teenage girls who were positive, had specific goals in mind, and good grades. It was the equivalent to the other beauty pageants locally, but specifically designed for African American teens simply because our community was always being shut out. I wanted very much to be involved in the pageant but at that stage in my life, I had a baby and would not have been allowed in. Nevertheless, the Jet magazines were definitely an inspiration to me and helped to shape me as a person and a woman.

Knowledge is the instrument used to open the windows of your soul

3

9705 Ash Street, the Molesting Begins

9705 SE Ash Street is the address of the house that I grew up in. It has very bad memories for me. The house was in Russellville in Southeast Portland, and the very first place of remembrance that I have of any type of molestation. It came from my stepbrother Colin Jr. He was a pretty stout person for his age. Eight and a half years older than me, Colin was somewhat of a bully. This would have been around 1960, so I was no more than five years old, but in my mind, he was old enough to know better. I don't have very pleasant memories of him either. He made me do things that, well, no stepbrother or brother should make a little girl do. He was the first molester.

It feels now like I'm becoming a target. Mother did not protect me from such evils. I'm sure she had no idea anything was even wrong. She only focused on what she did and did not want from us. I believe that she did not, nor could not, *feel* like a true mother. I believe she had no inner mothering nature because that truly does come from within.

After Colin Jr's dad and Mother divorced, Colin Jr went off with his dad, and then I think he lived with his natural mother Tina for a while. When Colin Jr got a little older, about fourteen or fifteen, he used to come by the house once in a while to see Mother and me. She, at that time worked the graveyard shift at the county hospital, now known as OHSU. So, sometimes she would be home and sometimes she wouldn't when he'd come by. She had given Colin permission to drop in and check on me from time to time at night, to make sure I was "safe". This was a really big mistake. That was like asking the fox to mind the henhouse. It was also when most of the molesting occurred.

Colin was about thirteen years old when he first started doing sexual things to me while he still lived in the house with me, like making me touch his penis and trying to sodomize me too.

The details are vivid, and have never left me. He would just show up and he would put me on top of him and put himself inside of me as much as he could without ripping my body open, which probably would have killed my extremely small framed body. It still makes me feel nasty and dirty and very embarrassed but it must be told. I never told Mother until I was probably age thirty. She had made me not trust her temperament because everything was always my fault. I began to resent her, and as I grew older, it became hard not to show that I was growing to not like her. I still allowed myself to do things for her, like give her mother's day gifts, cook for her, and when she got older, my husband and I even took her in and cared for her.

By then I had gotten saved and had forgiven her and Colin Jr. After all the years that went by, I never mentioned to Colin Jr that these acts never left me, nor have I forgotten how he hurt and humiliated me, and caused lifelong images of pain and embarrassment in my mind. I'm not sure why, but it's always been embarrassing for me to let the abusers know that I have not forgotten. To let them in on my "secret." The images will never go away, they continue to play in the back of mind, and I suppose they will continue to stay with me for the rest of my days.

That house that I grew up in on Ash Street was a place where the lifelong horrible memories began. But they don't end there. The very house seemed cold, and not belonging. It was something that Colin Sr and Mother had purchased together. They added a room in the back, which was my room. It had a small laundry room that looked like it had been built by them as well. I remember hating that house not only because of the things that Colin Jr did to me there but also because of what it stood for. No love, grown people fighting and arguing, divorce, and slave day on Saturdays. This meant get my behind out of bed early to help with huge washing of the clothes then hanging them outside on the line with clothespins if the weather was nice. If it was bad weather I'd have to hang them inside throughout the house on clothes lines, then dust the furniture sweep, mop, and buff the floors. It seemed the day was never going to end. All the housework had to be done in one full day and if I didn't do it right or just like she taught me, the extension cord would meet my body. As I got a little older, my add on jobs were dish washing and ironing starched clothes. She used the old fashioned heavy starch that you had to cook then hang dry and sprinkle down the clothes with water because when the clothing dried they were like corn flakes. Then, it had to be balled up in a nice round ball so that they would stay damp and ready to be ironed over a period of maybe a couple of days, depending on how many pieces we had. When she taught me the technique for ironing, I don't know how many times I got in trouble for not doing it just right, but with lots of practice, the technique finally came together of ironing a starched shirt or dress until it stood up by itself. That certainly is one chore that I learned quickly to hate among other things.

I do have a few good memorable times in my childhood years that were pleasant. Like when we used to go to her niece's Pearl's house for Christmas or for Thanksgiving dinner or they would come to ours. Pearl and JD had six children. One boy and the rest girls. We all were very close. I even taught their youngest daughter how to ride a bike. I must have been about eleven or twelve and she was about six or seven years old. I remember having so much fun teaching Charletta how to ride that bike and she never forgot that day. Maria, her third oldest was about two years older than me so she and I were very close. We did a lot of recording, singing and taping when we all would get together on some Sundays and almost all of the holidays. Us kids would usually have a good time with Mother's old (but within its time) reel-to-reel tape recorder that we used to mess around with. That's probably how and why I got so interested in recording, music and singing. Music and singing was so much fun. I remember saying to myself on more than one occasion that I wanted to be a famous singer and a nurse. Both of those childhood desires have been somewhat fulfilled. During this time, Colin Jr was in and out of trouble a lot. I'm not quite sure what exactly was going on in his life by now, but he did not mess with me anymore.

As time went on, the next time that I was a target for perverse sexual evils, happened not too long after Colin Jr molested me. We were visiting Laura, the sister of one of Mother's new boyfriends. Laura had a son who was fourteen years old at the time. While the grown ups were all chatting in the living room Timmy and I were in his bedroom, where the grownups sent me to so that I wouldn't be so bored in the room with them and they could talk freely.

We all had become almost like family, I thought. Laura, had babysat me before, she was like a mom figure to me. She sold Avon products, and I believe she's one of the reasons that I like makeup, lipstick, and beautifying myself today because she'd let me look at her books and let me play with her samples. I was very interested in that kind of stuff.

That night, while I was in his room, her son was teaching me grown up stuff like kissing and sticking his finger inside me until I bled. He pleaded with me not to tell, I walked out of his room very slowly and went back into the living room where the grown ups were.

Apparently my face said it all. His mother said, "what's wrong?" I said "nothing" because that was always my answer for almost everything. But they kept prying and asking me what's wrong? Well, finally they figured out what was wrong because I wasn't saying anything. Mother knew from my silence what was wrong. They began to get loud and fussing. Then Timmy got in big trouble because they suddenly realized that he had molested a six year old child.

Mother on the other hand, blamed me and said that I should have never been in his room. Basically justifying him and in so many words, saying it was my fault for being in his room, the room that *they* sent me to. The grownups took me to the hospital to see what kind of, if any, damage was done. I don't know what the diagnosis or prognosis was, but I do know that I got a very, very bad beating for it. For me, this was the beginning of not trusting Mother when she said, "tell me the truth and I won't whip you." Well, each time I'd tell her the truth, she darn near mutilated tiny me.

I believe God made me tough, physically, to be able to endure the massive cruel and brutal beatings that Mother would inflict upon me. He must have made me tough to endure the onslaught of physical corruption that took place on my very young and innocent body, as well as my mind.

I do not know exactly what Mother's problem was but I have some theories. Maybe in her mind she originally had good intentions, but then she would let her anger get in the way of her thinking. Possibly somewhere deep down inside she wanted someone to take care of her financially, she wanted a fine home, and she wanted a couple of perfect kids to complete the picture. Colin and I were far from perfect. She wanted the American Dream. Everything was opposite of what her ideals were. She had no clue on how to nurture children. She did not know or could not "feel" how to be motherly. No clue on how to effectively encourage me. No clue on how to say "I am proud of your work." Or "keep trying, don't give up." It was probably because maybe her mother never showed it to her or perhaps because she had no father in her life. She left home and got married at sixteen years old. Mother had to work very hard before marriage and all during her marriages and of course, after her divorces. But she really had been pinned down with me after she and Colin Sr divorced because now she would become the sole supporter of me, which maybe she resented. She had been married three other times before taking me from Mississippi. Mother was married a total of five times to try and find that *good* husband who would take care of her, which she found in husband number five. He ended up being the only earthly father that I really knew. So all of these things, I believe, played a factor in her abuses to me. Mother never came to grips with it, nor owned up to it, and since her passing in 2003, the healing process for me is still not totally complete. Instead it is ongoing and probably lifelong.

A girly girl, that was me, always playing with dolls, trying to sing, always in the mirror and playing with my hair. Mother was seeing another new boyfriend named David. He was a tall, sort of big guy. Of course when you're little everybody is big to you. He was one of the boyfriends that Mother went out with when she and Colin Sr divorced.

One of those times while playing in the mirror, I saw Dave's reflection. He was whispering "come here I want to tell you something." I froze staring at him in the mirror. Mother was asleep on the couch. This happened a few times on different occasions. I did not go to him but he eventually crossed the line and came into my room, took me in his arms and tried to kiss me as if I were a grown woman while I was squirming trying to get away. I was around seven years old by then. I still remember his nasty smelling breath and the nastiness of his tongue on my face as I was squirming to get loose.

Of course, Mother had said before that if anyone ever tried to bother me or touch me in any way, that I could tell her. That was not true. I never told her about it because I did not want to get beat again for something that was not my fault. So I suppressed it. And kept on suppressing it. All the abuses that ever took place were kept from her because *I* would have been beaten, or who knows, maybe even killed.

It is a very hurtful thing when someone who is supposed to be your nurturer tells you that "you ain't nothing and you will never be anything". Who says that to a child? Even though they are just words, they cut to the core. A small child who hears that enough is bound to start believing it. We all know that children are like little magnets and sponges, they pick up everything that you say and sometimes, even things that you do. They do not know how to guard their little spirits and protect themselves from hurt.

From the moment of the first molesting, I remember like it was yesterday, I knew that the blame would be on me. By the time Timmy Thompson molested me at age six and Mother beat me unmercifully, I knew then that she would never, ever believe anything I had to say about anything. I knew that she would never believe that her beloved boyfriends would even remotely think of putting their hands on me in that way. But they did.

At least one of them waited until I was about fourteen to try and force himself on me. The key word is *try*. It was the uncle of Timmy, who kept the friendship between he and Mother all of those years. Junior was an old boyfriend of hers but he was quite a bit younger by about twenty years. Yes, Mother would have been considered a cougar in her day. Even when she got married to her fifth husband, Lonnie, she and Junior kept the friendship but years later, he had his eye on younger women, including me.

I remember him coming over to the house one day while Mother was gone and Lonnie was most likely out of town on the road. I did not suspect that Junior, of all people would try something like that knowing that his own nephew had damaged me when I was little.

When he came to the house, like he did sometimes when Lonnie was on the road, I let him know that there was no need to come in because Mother was not home. He barged in and was going to try and rape me. I had to physically fight him off and he finally gave up and left. If Mother had known that, she would have blamed me. If she blamed me at age six, she most assuredly would have blamed me now.

~Reflections~

I have tried to picture what my life would have been like if Mother had not taken the trip to Mississippi that year, if she had not heard that her first cousin in the next county was giving her children away, and if she had decided not to take me from the ravages of poverty. What if she had discouraged Layla from giving her youngest child at that time away, stopping her from further breaking the bonds between me and my siblings and our biological mother? Chances are that Layla would have given me to someone else. I believe she was trying to "get rid" of the pain and trauma that she had endured by having all these children, who had been fathered by her stepfather.

I also have often wondered why Jesus stood by and allowed a small child to endure the tremendous and traumatic pain and suffering that my tiny frame endured for so many years. As a younger woman, I have had dreams, almost like a vision, of seeing Him standing, over me or more like hovering over me and watching the whole ordeal take place. He was preparing me for something. I recognize the rebellion and contempt that I felt for so long within my spirit for all the years of torture and pain inflicted on me by other people. I have no doubt that the verbal abuse had worn on my nerves and my spirit. Mother had pet degrading names for me like water head, cry baby and nappy head. Whoever said that sticks and stones would break your bones but words would never hurt, lied. Words do hurt. They cut to the core and they can also kill your spirit. I realize now why I cried so easily, my spirit was broken. If someone never has anything positive to say about you or to you and you have very little if any, encouragement, the self esteem is dramatically reduced to nothing. You begin to feel like the names that you are being called. It still saddens my heart when I think about all those times that I had to hear her yelling at me for no real reason. There was no reason at all to yell, I was not a loud, get in your way type of child. I learned to try and stay out of Mother's way but she focused extremely close on what I did wrong and not very much on the things that I did right. I remember my feelings being very easily hurt, even to look at me would cause me to cry. Mother would ask me, "what are you crying about?" I usually couldn't come up with a good enough answer as to why I was crying but it was largely because she had just got done yelling at me for something. So, of course, I would get in trouble again for crying for no reason. To this day, I still cannot stand to be yelled at and my feelings are still easily hurt. For this reason, I have to keep my heart and spirit guarded and protected. It is true that throughout this life of mine, there have been abuses, big upsets and emotional let downs from time to time. This has often caused depression at times and a nervous breakdown, which should not have happened at my young age of barely 30. I remember it quite vividly. A young adult full of life has no business having a nervous breakdown. My mind, body, and soul must have really been at its lowest point. There were several different things going on in my life at the time. Mother needed me to help her with the understanding of her diabetes that she had just been diagnosed with. I had a very stressful job at a nursing care facility plus a family to take care of. That year was also the height of baby momma drama, it all took its toll. Fortunately, I did not have to be hospitalized but I was back and forth to doctors and taking medicine. Rest, quietness and stability is what I really needed most and to let the past and some of the present go at that time. As a year or two went by, thank God I got better but still had to be careful and not let myself get too emotionally stressed. I personally believe it was due to all the traumatic buildup coupled with the new situations going on in my life.

I used alcohol as an escape mechanism. That was my drug of choice. Many times I had to be carried out of my own car to my bed from excessive drinking. For some reason, I never knew my limit. It scares me now to even think back on how I abused myself at times, but so glad that God waited for me to come to my senses. The beatings and cruelty inflicted on me is only a drop in the bucket for what He endured for all of us and He forgives us, still.

I realize now that in order for something to grow, something must die. Thank God I did not die physically, but in some ways every time a child gets abused, whether by getting beat unmercifully or being violated sexually, something in one's spirit dies. That "death" then takes on a different form. You can truly let yourself die inside by feeling shame, guilt, depression, worthlessness, and blame others for what you don't have, or what your life could have been, or, you can choose to live and help others live to.

Looking back, my childhood was horrible. The only birthday I remember celebrating was the celebration dinner that Mother's friend Mrs Miller made for both of us because her birthday was three days before mine. She was sweet like that. I think she knew that birthday celebrations were a rarity around our household. Mrs Miller would have been the one who I would give the credit to for placing in me the spirit of celebrating birthdays and making people feel special on their day. Having done that one act of birthday kindness says to me, you do matter and I'm glad you were born. You are special whether you know it or not. I've always felt that when your friends and family have very little regard for the day you were born, says to me, you matter very little, if at all. Sadly, some have wanted me to feel that way, even in childhood. Mrs Miller was a smoker and if I remember correctly, she left this earth with some sort of lung problem, it may have been cancer.

Her husband, Mr Miller, was one of the men who was in the predator group. He tried to be slick and subtle about it, but not slick enough. By the time I was probably about ten years old, it was growing more and more clear that most men were sexual perverts, at least in the world I was living in. I had no one to trust, not Mother, not the school, because they would tell her, not a sister or brother because they had been left in Mississippi, not even a best friend at that time, not one.

Sometimes we have to suffer many things to develop into the person we want to become

4

Making the Best of a Bad Situation

Lonnie, My Dad

My father, Lonnie, was the fifth and last husband that Mother had. He was a mild mannered man. He never had any children of his own either, although there had been some talk of him possibly being the father of a former girlfriend's child but if he had truly been the father, he was not the kind of man to shirk his responsibilities, in fact he welcomed responsibilities.

Lonnie was a very good provider. He worked as a dining car waiter, bartender and porter for the Union Pacific Railroad for about thirty five years. He probably would have worked longer if he had not fallen ill to emphysema, heart condition, and then lung cancer. Lonnie was established with his own stuff. He had already bought a house just big enough for him. It was a 2 bedroom cute home. I like to call it a bachelor home.

Apparently he didn't plan on marrying, at least no time soon. He had owned a couple of cars by the time he and Mother met. I believe he had an old Dodge and after that, he got a 1963 Dodge Dart. I always thought that first car was not the best looking thing that one could have, but he liked it. It's true, he was a Dodge man because later he would buy a brand new Dodge Dart in the early '70's and that car would be the car to start me driving.

Lonnie was a native Texan. He came from a line of mostly educators, and nurses. That was his goal for me, to go to nursing school and become a registered nurse. When Lonnie and Mother got married I was eleven years old.

I'm not exactly sure why they waited until he had a heart attack when I was fourteen, to adopt me. Whatever the deciding factor was, it's fair to say that he wanted to make sure that he wasn't getting a spoiled little tyrant of a brat who was going to carry his name or that didn't care too much for him.

It was quite the opposite. We had a good father/daughter relationship. He taught me a lot about the business field, which I have used from that day until now. Lonnie was extremely smart and he liked to drink beer and smoke cigarettes. He finally gave up the cigs just before he had to go on oxygen in the last stages of lung cancer. He must have smoked for about forty years, since his military days. He and Colin Sr treated me more like a daughter than Mother or any of her boyfriends ever had. The difference was, Colin Sr left us and Lonnie stuck it out…until he got sick and eventually passed on in 1980.

I believe Lonnie's reason for adopting me was so that if anything should happen to him he wanted to make sure his wife and daughter were financially taken care of. I remember a conversation we had about mother on the telephone once during his illness. He said to me, 'I wish you and your mother could get along better'. I told him, "Lonnie, mother and I have never gotten along and we probably never will". During that same process of adopting me, they allowed my first name to also be legally changed from Marlena to Margaret. I always hated the name Marlena. It sounds so unthought out, common and weak, which is the very opposite of what I am. Even though a lot of my family still calls me that name, they know what my preference is. So at fourteen years of age, Lonnie would adopt me to give me a more solid foundation should anything happen to him. Ironically, when my father passed away some ten years later, Mother did exactly the opposite.

Intentions are the things that can help determine if you will help or hurt something or someone

5

My Spiritual Foundation

THE one thing that I do appreciate Mother for is the fact that she always made sure that I was clean and well dressed with patent leather shoes to boot and hair very well kept. This was especially true when she'd send me to Sunday school. She made sure that I went to Sunday school every Sunday. Mother always made sure that I had a handkerchief with some change tied up in it to put in the Sunday school plate. The church was a small traditional Pentecostal church on the corner of where we lived in Russellville. The area was predominantly white with a small but close-knit community of black families. Everyone knew each other and helped each other out. For the ones that went to church, Mt Calvary is the church they went to. Sister Johnson and Brother Bagley were my regular Sunday school teachers. Sister Johnson was one of the Mother's of the church. She had a very sweet spirit, so kind, nurturing and giving. I believe, at that time, she was the only one saved in her home, and she was faithfully in church every Sunday. She instilled so many good things in me, like helping me to find and memorize scriptures and read bible verses. She taught me and the other children what it meant to be a Christian and she taught me that Jesus loved me. They would give us a poem for the Easter program to memorize and recite in front of the whole church on Easter Sunday. I was always so scared to stand up in front of people and talk, or do anything in front of people, partly because being told so much that I couldn't do anything right and that I was ugly, so I felt ugly. I liked being in our children's choir but it was painful and traumatic to go before a crowd even though deep down inside I wanted to do it. These two people, Brother Bagley and Sister Johnson along with the help of Pastor Daniels, laid the spiritual foundation in me. Thanks also go to Mother, even through her abusing me she wanted to make sure that I had a solid spiritual foundation. I thank them all for that. Though I was a regular Sunday school attendee and Mother was more of an occasional attendee, none of her relatives or the church knew that any of the abuse was going on. I was in such fear to breathe a word to anyone, not even to my closest friend and relative, my cousin, Maria. I was in fear that it would get back to Mother, and if it did, I knew she would for sure kill me! So I hid it along with all the sexual abuse. After that incident with Timmy and getting the worst beating ever, I just didn't tell anymore when it happened. I felt that I was getting beat for enough stuff already like wetting the bed, getting some D's and F's on my report card, or lying about getting a snack from the kitchen then covering it up because she was adamant about always asking before getting anything out of the kitchen.

In some cases, freedom is a luxury not necessarily a way of life

6

Happier Times

In the kitchen, that was the one place that I really liked to be. I liked watching Mother whip up different foods, especially around the holidays. She would let me help her by getting different things or ingredients that she needed to go into whatever she was making at the time. One of my favorite things to watch her make was cornbread dressing along with sweet potato pies, which was my favorite pie growing up. I would watch Mother put out pie after pie sometimes she'd make as many as seven to nine pies mostly for us. She would give some to her niece and any nephews that dropped by. I would be her dressing taster to let her know if the dressing needed more salt, pepper or spices. She taught me the art of never having to measure anything and her motto was "a good cook doesn't need to measure anything." Well, I found out that she is right, I do prefer to just start with a little salt, pepper or spice, then just add and add some more if necessary until I get the results that I'm looking for. I did learn eventually that some things do actually need to be measured, but for the most part, I like her way better. For those times we spent together in the kitchen I am grateful because they were happy times and I make those same excellent cakes, pies, dressing and a whole variety of other foods that she used to make. My dad Lonnie, also taught me quite a few cooking techniques. It was enjoyable hanging around in the kitchen with him too, especially when he'd make oven barbecue and that spectacular tamale pie. In the early years of their marriage until he had the heart attack, he did most of the cooking when he was in town. He was probably more of a gourmet mixed with South Western flair type of cook. Mother was a straight up Southern cook, I had the best of both worlds in that respect. Little did I know, those times were preparing me to be a great cook like the both of them, if I do say so myself.

One of Mother's friends, Mrs. Diamond Kent, became a very close confidant of mine, but she and Mother were friends and I still feared Mother. Now that I was a young adult, I never even told her about the years of abuse from Mother. Miss Kent, as I called her, was a very short woman with a big presence. She and Mother had been friends since the early 1940's. She had seven grown children of her own with a host of grandchildren. Although she wasn't really a godly woman, she would become my Godmother. She gave me my own first bible with my name engraved on it when I was about fourteen years old after I got baptized in the Catholic Church, (well I should say sprinkled with water). When Lonnie and Mother got married he was Catholic at the time and talked Mother into having me convert to Catholicism even though she wouldn't convert. Miss Kent was very crafty with making different wines, canning her own pickles, pickling her own garlic, okra and whatever other veggie she thought of, along with making her own fudge. She'd get someone to drive her out to the fields (a lot of the time that would be me) and pick her own veggies to can or pickle, she'd pick her own dandelions and rose petals for her wines. She gave lots of good homemade items away at Christmas time and birthdays as gifts, very uniquely packaged I might add.

Miss Kent never rejected me, she spent so much valuable time with me. Sometimes we'd just talk and talk and talk. She took me to the movies, to restaurants, to the department stores and just showed me that she cared. She took me places Mother never did. Miss Kent and me were "road dogs." I don't remember her ever telling me that she loved me, but somehow I just knew.

By about age twenty she had taught me several things about life, like always stand up for what you believe in, and that you do have a right to be heard. She even gave me her recipe on how to make a cherry cream cheese cake, which is now and has been one of my signature recipes that I still use today and my husband, friends, and family love it. I probably wouldn't have learned how to broil a steak, or sear shrimp if it wasn't for her. She wanted to share her walnut fudge recipe with me but I wasn't so interested in that because it was too long of a process. I am proud to say that I actually taught her how to make homemade dumplings. She always loved my chicken and dumplings recipe (which I got from Mother), but Miss Kent did not master how to make and cut the dumplings until she watched me make them so much that she finally got the hang of it some years later. She would call me over several times a year to make and cut her a supply of dumplings so that she could freeze them and have them on hand. Even though I was grown, but not as grown as Miss Kent, that made me feel so special that a full fledged adult person actually liked something that I did.

In addition to many other things, love is a continuous well that never runs dry

7

A Marriage *Not* Made in Heaven

As I became an adult, my parents still liked to go to the dog track and the horse races. I grew up going to the track with them. Looking back, I realize that Mother used to lie about my age to get me in because children had to be twelve or older to get in, and at that time I must have been between nine and eleven years old. No child under twelve could get in without a parent. The dog racetrack officials made it a rule because so many little kids were always running around loose and wild while the parents were busy playing the numbers. Mother had instilled, if nothing else, a good and well disciplined behavior in me. If I had even thought about acting wild like some of the other kids did at the track, I'm sure I would have gotten beat right then and there! Anyway, because I was so well behaved and she was friendly with the sheriff and the guys at the entrance gate, even though I was a very small child, she was passing me off as twelve and getting away with it. Of course, there was a time she almost had an altercation on the elevator with someone about my age and Mother told him off and didn't think twice about it. He shut up real quick.

I remember that during my years of going to the race track with them, I became fully trained and knew how to go up to the window for Mother and place bets for her and on occasion walked around to people watch. Well, I ran into a man who caught my eye in a very profound way. He was almost jet black with smooth silky skin and he wore all black. He was sporting a couple of gold teeth, which I happened to know was a Southern Black trademark and tradition. I thought it was absolutely beautiful. I passed by like I didn't see him, but definitely liked that quiet but strong demeanor he had. Every time now when we'd go to the races, I would purposely look for him. Then, it happened. He finally did notice and he approached me and asked me what my name was. We formally introduced ourselves. He told me his name was James Lance but his friends called him Jimmy. He was mysterious and quiet. Strong and he knew I was very, very young because I told him. When he told me how old he was, which was not his true age, I was flabbergasted to say the least. He didn't tell me his true age until probably several months into our long relationship. He was a lot older than me and I knew it but didn't really care about that. Looking back, I believe a strong father figure was what my spirit was looking for. Someone to take care of me, to comfort and take me away from the cares of this world. Trust me, it proved to not be him!

I suppose your first love is one of those things that you never really forget. At the beginning of our relationship, I was so intrigued with this much older man, it seemed I was just so drawn to him and wanted to see him every chance I could get. Mother had such a tight rein on me until it was almost impossible to get to see him. So I did what any other normal teenager would have done, I skipped school several times and played like I was going to my friend's house then call him to have him meet me. Of course, there were still our meetings at the dog and horse races. I don't really know whose fault it was that Jimmy and I got together, whether it was my inner need to have that father figure that was missing as a little child growing up or his greedy and selfish need to have a young innocent virgin. It doesn't really matter. What matters is the years that would follow were very turbulent and grew to be often times violent.

Our secret relationship went on for a year. A high school student with about above average grades, a very good job after school and during the summer which, if I had stayed on with that particular company, it would have paid for a full scholarship for my college education to come back after college and still work for them. That was an offer I should not have messed up. Instead, I got pregnant with my first child. I was so very distraught about it; my body and mind wasn't mentally, physically or emotionally ready to have a child. Well my daughter was born at the end of August going into my senior year of high school. Needless to say that during my whole junior year of school, I was pregnant. No one knew except my best friend Martha Pierce and my parents. I did not even start to show until June of my junior year, by then school was almost out for the summer.

There were many turns and twists during my junior year of high school. I was always sick, it was so hard to get out of bed to get to school. Neither Mother nor Lonnie took me to school, I still had to get that bus every morning. You know it was business as usual. Just because I was knocked up didn't mean I would get any special privileges. In fact, quite the opposite. They talked about sending me to some school for "pregnant girls". They mentioned putting me out and no baby was going to come into their house. It felt like I was always under the gun so to speak. Early on when they initially found out about Jimmy, they had gone to the district attorney to try and press charges against him for statutory rape. The only thing that saved him was me. Of course they all tried to put pressure on me to go against him and testify but it was just as much my fault as his. I was no baby and knew full well right from wrong. So during the pregnancy he was very supportive but by now he had fallen into a life of scandalous behavior to try and make money the quick fast way. I realized that I had gotten away clean with being pregnant and the school not finding out in my junior year.

Back then, the school would put any girl out if they knew she was pregnant. I decided that no way was I going to be a statistic of another young unwed African American female being a high school dropout. So my baby was born in August and I went right into my senior year in September and on to complete and to take that walk across the stage of The Civic Auditorium with my graduating class, and some years later on to college.

Jimmy was a very kind, quiet sort of guy when we met. For about the first three years of our relationship things went well during that time. He was a laborer at the city's Shipyard and that kind of job has layoffs quite often. Well needless to say, he was getting laid off a lot. He began to turn more and more to making money the quick way by dealing drugs. Ritalin was the hot item back then. Later it escalated to cocaine. Oddly enough he never tried to introduce me to any of the stuff he was smoking or selling or inhaling. Thank God he didn't. What things I did try, were tried later on my own with no help from him. He started out at first just selling part time, only when necessary. I think he actually still had a consciousness for people. He wasn't finding any work, and continued to be laid off, so the selling and the occasional drink got to be more and more and heavier and heavier. He used to make his own runs out of town to pick up his shipments. On one of his short runs coming back from California, something terrible happened. I got a call while still living at my parent's home with my young daughter. It was the hospital in Eugene, Oregon.

On the night of our daughter's first birthday, Jimmy had an accident, an almost fatal car accident. Mother asked her nephew's friend if he could drive us to Eugene. So he did. We got to the hospital and there he was, Jimmy, lying there in a hospital bed with a freshly amputated right arm. I was in shock and disbelief. 18 years old, a new mother, a young mother and this man whom I said I loved, with a very noticeable altered look.

✦✦✦

As time went on Jimmy eventually was transported to Portland, and I would later move in with him. We had gotten an apartment just before his run to California, before the car accident. It was there that I started noticing his mood and mannerism had changed towards me. It wasn't too drastic at first, but still a change. He went back to his same old lifestyle of street selling but with a twist. He was developing his own drug habit, which now I realize that he probably had gotten hooked on painkillers from that accident and moved to his own substance that he was selling. I don't know, I only know that he grew increasingly violent towards me.

I stayed in the apartment with him for about three months then moved back home. The next time I left home and moved in with him again we were married and moved into a two bedroom house. There I experienced the most traumatizing time of my young adult life. When he'd leave at night he would booby trap the front and back doors and windows so that he would be able to tell if I had let someone in or out. One night he came in and just wanted a reason to jump on me. He accused me of letting a neighbor guy in the house. He grabbed me and forced me over to the front window and told me in a very forceful loud voice, "look, now this guy is standing in the window naked waiting for you." I looked and no one was standing anywhere. Jimmy had grown psychotic. He then decided he would use me for target practice, at least make me think he was going to shoot me. He got a gun from somewhere hidden in the house, I ran into the bathroom and locked the door. Everything was quiet, my daughter was asleep. By this time, I didn't know what was happening so I cracked the door and looked out, and there he was propped over the television aiming the small pistol at me, but he didn't shoot it. I darted across the hall into my room, yelling which woke up my two year old daughter. She came into the room and climbed into my lap. Jimmy came in there ranting, raving, and threatening me while now loading a 30x30 magnum with one hand. This big gun doesn't have regular bullets it has shells the size of railroad spikes. I was petrified. As he pointed it at me while my daughter sat in my lap, I looked into the face of death.

∽∂∽

Jimmy had his finger on the trigger pointing it directly at me and telling me "if you don't tell me where that honky is, I'll blow you off the face of this earth." Needless to say, there was no one in the house besides him, our two year daughter and me. I kept telling him that. I managed to call Mother on the telephone after he went into the living room but before he yanked the cord out of the wall. She came out and tried to get me to go home with her but I stayed. She said, "Well let me take the baby" so I did. I'm sure it was the grace of God that did not let that Magnum go off. Strangely enough he went to sleep and I slept very lightly.

The next day we got up apparently still fuming from the night before. I was sure that I was ready for this fight now. He was going to leave so I threw all of his nice clothes, suits and everything, outside onto the wet and dewy ground. He said in a threatening low key tone "all my shit better be back in my closet when I get back." Then he got into his very exquisite long black on black Caddy and attempted to back out. By now, I'm in my older red Mercury attempting to run into his Caddy. This happened twice, Jimmy then pulled his car forward one last time, parked and flew into the house, I'm sure he was angered to the max. I then flew in behind him, just as I was about to step in through the door, he grabbed me and pulled me in and we fought like cats and dogs. After tussling for a few minutes he pinned me down and hit me on the side of my head with the butt of a handgun, busting my ear open. This stunned my hearing of course. I remember seeing blood splatter and it took several minutes for my head to stop spinning and my ear to stop ringing. I couldn't hear that good for a long while after that. Of course, I called Mother once again on that phone that he had yanked out before, which I thought was broken. I told her what happened and she came out again. As she was coming up that Glisan Street hill, he was going down the hill. When she came inside my house, I noticed she was carrying her purse like it was a little heavy. Mother did own a .38 revolver and if need be, I believe she would have used it.

She took me to the doctor to get my ear stitched up and the doctor made some kind of wise crack comment like "when are you gonna leave him, when he kills you?" I told him to mind his own damn business and just finish fixing my damn ear. Even though I didn't like what he had said, I knew he was right. I soon acted on that comment by getting my cousin to help me move almost all the furniture over to my parents' garage. Not one piece of furniture had I bought but I knew that by Jimmy being a man, he would be able to start over better than me and I would also be the one raising our daughter.

After that move, I filed for divorce and didn't think twice about "getting anything". All I wanted was my little car, my baby and the furniture that I had already taken. He could keep his Caddy, his money and the house that he just made a down payment on previously which was not all that. I had had enough of this mess and just wanted out.

By the time my twentieth birthday came, I had become a wife, mother, and a divorcee` (not necessarily in that order.) At twenty, most kids are still living at home under their parent's wings. But none of this stopped me from later going on and graduating from college while venturing out into the work force full time as well. Sure, like a lot of people, I can look back and think to myself that if I could change some things, or at least the order of some things, my life would be different. But even though a lot of these events were unhealthy and very often violent, it helped build compassion and concern for others.

In 2004, Jimmy passed away. I'm not sure what the cause of death was but one thing is for sure, it was the end of another tragic era. Although we had long since gone our separate ways, when I heard of his passing I couldn't help but to remember for a moment, some of the times that we had together. Most were not good times or happy times but they were times that helped to yet shape my senses to the real world. It was because of his brutality and ultimately our divorce that would propel me into being self reliant, and later, try to instill that lesson into the children that would be entrusted in my care. It would have been a great sense of accomplishment if this lifelong valuable lesson was one hundred percent successful.

Life, an ever changing learning curve with a lot of rocky roads, hills, bumps and valleys...but then there's the mountain top

8

Real Love *and* the Breakup

No one really expects to find real love when you've just gotten out of a turbulent and in the latter years violent relationship and bitter divorce. Of course, after my divorce had finalized I dated a few guys who appeared to have their lives together and under control but no doubt I was wrong. One guy, Paul, whom I probably could have fallen in love with, let me catch him with his baby's momma, in bed. I mean, who gives someone a key to their house and tells them they are welcome to drop in anytime, which I did, just for the heck of it this one morning in particular while on my way to work. To my surprise he's laying up in bed with the baby's momma! My first instinct was to start slicing and dicing--both of them!

I had seen her before at his house. He had, at that time, reassured me that they only had the baby (who was three years old) in common, nothing more. That was a downfall of mine, I believed too easily. But I kept my cool, and while he calmly acted like nothing was wrong, telling me "hey how you doing" and "this is not what it looks like"….which I might add, further aggravated me because now he's trying to take me for a *complete* fool and insult my intelligence. I did an about face never saying a word, leaving them wondering, 'what is on her mind'? I had not really experienced how men could lie to your face and sound so convincing, and although Jimmy and I did not get along later in the relationship, I never "caught" him with other women and as far as I knew, he did not make it a practice to lie to me, and I never caught him in a lie. The guys I was meeting was close to my own age. The oldest being about six years older than me. Apparently that was not old enough for me. I knew that I was out of my league with these younger guys because, as mentioned before my personality was drawn to older men. The older ones usually knew and understood how to treat women. They have more of an appreciation for women, in my opinion. So needless to say, Paul and I did not stay together. Then one night while out at the "place where friends meet" that's what the motto was at Geneva's Lounge. You could go there on Saturday night to get your groove on in a packed house or during the week just to hang out. Well this was one of those hang out nights for me. I went alone and always had enough money to buy myself at least one drink and sip on it for a long while. I happened to notice a high school friend named Jackie Mae and her husband sitting at the next table. Jackie Mae saw me and invited me over to sit with them. There had been a particular man that I noticed a few times before but didn't really think anything of it. Well, I saw this guy again that night sitting alone at a table and like before, didn't think anything of it. Little did I know, this man not only knew my friend whom I was sitting with but that he and I had so much in common. Who knew that twelve years later he would become my husband, soul mate, friend and father to most of my children but it would prove to be a long and sometimes bumpy road...

That night my high school friend Jackie Mae formally introduced Calvin Roberts and me. He asked very smoothly if he could join us. As I remember it, Jackie Mae gave me the look like "it's up to you girl." My face no doubt was saying to her, "fine with me." We told him yes he could join us. After having a couple of bottles of champales (which was my drink of choice for hanging out during the week), we danced, laughed and enjoyed the night away.

Calvin was tall, slim and good looking, a little under the weight that I liked but I figured he's got so much other stuff going for him I was willing to overlook the weight requirement. We decided to go to my place to continue to enjoy the presence of each other's company. After we got into my car, I started having second thoughts about letting Calvin come to my house or even being in the car with me, sort of turning schitzo on him. I thought to myself, what are you doing! You don't even know this man. He could be a serial killer, a rapist or just about anything. Keep in mind also that I was a little tipsy, to say the least. I told him that I had changed my mind, and that he had to get out of the car. He was like, "why did you change your mind, we had a good time." I said "yeah but I don't know you, just get out" and I started demanding that he get out of my car. Somehow he managed to make me understand that he was a nice guy. He let me know he is not going to "try anything" he just wanted to get to know me better. He was nothing but a true gentleman from the time we met. I really liked the person in him, so off to my apartment we went.

We had so much fun talking, getting to know each other and finding out that the one major thing that we had in common was music, the universal language. I always loved to play my records, sing and record my voice. Calvin was a musician, he played keys, organ, and piano. As we talked, and played with the song Sara Smile on the voice recorder, we were finding out a little more about each other. That song became one of our signature songs that would help to define just how we felt about each other. Calvin had been honest with me from the start. He told me that he was living with someone but that the relationship was pretty much in turmoil. I was relieved to know that he was not married.

The next few years were good at times and very turbulent at times too. Mainly because of our lifestyles and the decisions we were making. He wanted or perhaps needed more than one woman. I, of course would tell him that he was the only man, knowing full well that he wasn't, after all, why should I commit to just him and he wouldn't or couldn't commit to only me? This type of behavior went on for several years and no doubt it caused us to argue, fight and eventually break up for more than a year. We were young and both of us very hot headed but were deeply in love with each other. We would rather fight than switch. Oh there were times that we had small breakups and we'd go back together, but when we broke up this time, I thought that was truly the end of our hot relationship. Even after finding out I was pregnant, I still didn't think we would get back together. I just knew that there would be Calvin and me no more.

Time can be your best friend if used wisely or your worst enemy if not used wisely

9

Rejection, a Fierce Fury

THIS thing called rejection has always been with me. It makes me feel like the whole world is against me, when the whole world doesn't even know me. The first time I really realized what this thing was that I felt, and recognized what it was, I must have been in the second grade. I knew I felt it at home. That's probably why I got beat so severely, this was mother's way of regretting her decision to bring me from Mississippi, therefore resenting and rejecting me. Rejection comes in many forms, sometimes through so called friends and even through church, unfortunately.

Everyone wants friends and everyone wants to be accepted; if we are not accepted and don't have outlets it can cause uncertainty, disillusionment and depression. Some people just seem to have people around them all the time, or have a few significant friends who you know will call you whenever anything is going on and just keep you in the loop of things. Or, perhaps you might be that person on someone's list of people to call first instead of being the very last to call, if at all. It was a little different for me.

It is so wonderful if one has a friend who not necessarily knows all of your business, but who has your back and you have theirs, and you know you never have to worry whether this friend will be your friend through life's ups and downs; through marriages and divorces; through good times and bad times; just always waking up knowing that even if you're in a most perfect relationship with the man of your dreams, that you can still count on that friend, and one of you will call the other at least every couple of days. A friendship that has no jealousy, and if it does crop up, it can be talked out. A friendship that will not allow one to cross the line and try to take the other one's man or husband.

That is the kind of friend that I was and would have been and still can be, and would have loved it if I had that kind of real friend. A true friend, one who no matter what, will not reject you.

❦

Some years later after getting saved, I got in the choir at church. It was a blessing, but something happened that just didn't set right with me. After being in the choir for probably about a year, I got sick with bronchitis and was out for about six weeks. We all had a phone list and some of us knew each other pretty well. Maybe I had too great of an expectation for the group, but for some reason I just felt that if you're involved with a group of people every week and sometimes a couple of times a week that when someone is out, somebody should make a phone call to at least try to find out if that person is dead or alive. I didn't get that one phone call. That made me so distraught that I had decided to just not get back involved in the choir.

When I was finally able to go back to church, the choir director said to me "why didn't you call us, we would have prayed for you?" It was behooving to me to call while being so sick.

I was also involved in a women's group that was not the best suited for me. Some things I got blamed for were not my fault. I shared my feelings with someone else in confidence about something that went on in one of the women's meetings that directly involved me that I did not agree with and it got back to one of the pastors and really blew up. That whole experience taught me three things: a) Just because someone says they are saved or even a churchgoer, doesn't mean they fully practice the doctrine that Jesus taught, to love one another, to help one another especially those that are in the House of Faith or fellow Christians. b) To be even more cautious about who I'm talking to especially "church folks." Not everyone wants to be your "sister" or "brother" and not everyone is sanctified. c) Even if someone says they forgive you, in my opinion, very rarely do they *really* forgive you. They say "yes I forgive you" but you can still feel that they have not really let it go, you can tell they do not want to start anew and you're still an outcast. So it's all just lies. After having a meeting or two with some of the people involved, I was not one of the *sisters* anymore. No one said it, but I could *feel* it.

As a result of this woman breaking my confidence and going to one of the pastors, no women could have any meetings or hold women's groups under the umbrella of the church unless it was ok'd before hand by the church, which in my opinion, should have been like that from the get go. So, needless to say, I was now an outcast. Even though they said everything was ok, I just kind of knew that it wasn't, especially when some of the women stop speaking to me, in the church building no less. I never got contacted, called or invited anymore…to anything. It hit me so hard I allowed it to throw me into a great depression.

Rejection hits not only among the church people but also within families believe it or not. This kind of thing happens within my own family, I have asked certain family members to forgive me for whatever wrong they feel I've done to them and they have said "yes I'll forgive you" (even though they still don't own up to the fact that they were not easy to be around some of the time.) But the forgiveness was just empty words. I look at it as a life long abuse pattern and them saying secretly, "I want to be mad at her because now if I act like I really forgive her, I'll have to do good towards her." Rejection, to me can also be when you are the last to know about *anything* but usually the first to be blamed for almost everything. The Lord did strengthen and heal me from that anger and mistrust once again of people, especially women. It seems this fiery fury has always been around in my life in one form or another. But He has taught me to go on, and when I have done all, just stand.

Never lose sight of who you are and what you have endured to get to where you haven't been

10

I Want My Sisters

If you have at least one sister, cherish her. While my brothers are very important, my sisters are extremely important to me, especially since I have always known that I have them. If you have an older sister she should be like an extension of a mother figure. She should have the wisdom, care and concern the same way a mom would. If you have a younger sister then you become the nurturer because you are now the eldest of the two. Both can certainly be not only sisters but also close friends.

That is exactly what I have wanted all of my life... for Mary Ana, Lutricia, Audra, Penny and myself to be. Realizing that we are all in our fifties and sixties now, this has not happened yet. All but one of them is older than I. And while I love them all, and have tried to sustain a relationship with them all, there has been over the years very little reciprocation from them.

I feel that we are life strangers and will probably be just that for the rest of our lives. They were raised together for some of their young lives but you might say I'm the "black sheep" of the bunch. We all know that the bonds were severed; even so, it seems to me that love would have caused them to consistently reach back to me, to be at least a close friend and try a little harder to reach back.

There is in my soul still a pronounced sadness, a burning hole in my heart for my sisters. Oh, how I have often longed for a tight knit bond with my siblings. Over the years I have even taken friends as sisters to fill the void of not being close with my own blood sisters. Of course, it never worked out because women seem to be far more fickle than men, and very quick to write you off when you say or do something that ticks them off. It's amazing to me that they contact each other from time to time, but it feels like a big struggle to stay consistently in touch with me. This too seems like a blatant disregard and a form of rejection.

I missed out on the childhood memories that they all can share with each other like their little singing group called The Cantrell Sisters and going to the store together buying candy and Lutricia making them give up their candy to her if she wanted it. And just doing things that sisters do. These are stories that I've heard just in these past few years. It would have been nice to have my sisters around so that I could share in those childhood memories with them.

It would be nice to have my sisters around right now to share in holiday dinners, birthdays, girl talk and family vacations occasionally with each other. Just writing about it makes me get misty eyed. Mary Ana has started to try to make a move to stay in contact with me, but has yet to make a move to come to where I am. It is my hope and prayer that one day we all can come back together whole heartedly and bond. As long as we are still living and breathing it is never too late. After all, now that we are adults, bonding becomes a conscious decision, just like anything else. The first and last time we all were together at the same time in the same place was September 2002 at Layla's funeral, forty five years after I had been given away, how truly, truly sad. I realize that it does take effort to accomplish anything in life.

I further realize that everyday life just happens; people are on the go working, taking care of children, husbands, boyfriends or whatever, and it may take a real effort and commitment to keep in touch with someone whom you have not had a bond with. It also takes love. Love is the key to so many, many things in life. It should not matter if we all have a bond or not, just the fact that I am their sister should be enough. When I hear or read about stories of other peoples lives on how they found their sibling or a lost parent after they have grown up, just makes me always cry. These people find each other and never let go. They actually get it. I often find myself rejoicing inside, right along with them, when they find that given away child, or that missing parent. In 2001, I was on a mission to finally see my oldest sister in Phoenix, Arizona. After speaking to her only a few times on the telephone over the years, something inside me, said it's time now, she is not going to come to you, so it's time you go to her. My husband was in total agreement with it. That Thanksgiving, I made the bulk of the Thanksgiving dinner for my family and took off for Arizona. My sister, one of her sons and one of her daughters, and her little grandson greeted me and welcomed me with open arms. I wasn't sure how I would recognize her but I was sure to recognize her when I heard her speak. She had told her daughter that she would know me anywhere, and she did. When I first saw my eldest sister, I knew that it was her, but it was sealed when she opened her mouth and said, "there's my sister, girl I don't know what to say"! I knew this was Mary Ana. She looked almost exactly like my brother Wendell in female version. Wendell and I had seen each other as recent as 2000. When Calvin and I took a trip to Alabama, Wendell had drove over from Mississippi to spend some time with us and to finally meet his brother-in-law, Calvin, in person. Before that I hadn't seen him in twenty years nor the rest of my siblings. The rest of Mary Ana's family accepted me with open arms, all of my nieces and nephews, my brother-in-law, Jarvis, treated me like we all had not lost any time at all. It was a truly remarkable feeling. Finally a real sense of what a blood sister, nieces, nephews,

brother-in-laws and most of all a big sister feels like.
The only word that comes close to describing the feeling, is P R I C E L E S S.

Everything has a meaning and a purpose, especially time

11

The Reconciliation

It was late spring, early summer when it happened, although Calvin had only dropped in on me a few times during our breakup, just to say hello he claimed. I actually thought he was stopping by to gloat and show me what I had lost. I must admit he did always look fine and fly when he'd come around. Calvin was always a gentleman and very popular with the ladies but this, apparently was one lady he could not forget about, no matter what the reason for our breakup.

A few months after my second child was born, I moved into my parent's rental house and Calvin started coming over there to see me. We had a few intimate moments and he made a startling suggestion, announcement or whatever you want to call it. He announced that we both knew that we loved each other and if I wanted to, we could get back together and "see what it be like". During that time there was another guy in my life that I had been kicking it with. Thad was an ok guy, he wanted to take care of my children and me but I did not love him. I was totally honest with him about Calvin. I sent Thad on his way, and of course he was very angry with me. He said that Calvin would end up leaving me, which ironically, Mother put it another way. She said that if you let a man lay up with you, he will never marry you. But of course, they both proved to be wrong.

Now, I was ready to begin a whole new chapter in my life with Calvin and my little family...little did I know, it was not going to be that simple. Me and Calvin's relationship was often times very tumultuous and sometimes violent, to say the least. We were very possessive of each other. Like I said earlier, we would rather fight than switch. Our lifestyles often got us into compromising situations, however, we stayed together, fought it out, worked it out and later God threw it out.

God's work was just beginning when Calvin recommitted his life back to Christ before we got married. One good thing after another started happening. When God began to work on Calvin, it spilled over on to me. I got reclaimed, graduated from business college then after a devastating miscarriage the Lord blessed us with our last child, another son. I made a conscious decision to give up smoking, which was a big issue with me. I had quit a few times before. Once I stopped for three weeks, and another time I quit for a whole year and picked it back up just to see "if I could still inhale." But this time when I quit, somehow I knew it was going to be for good. It was the Holy Spirit tugging on me. It was God drawing me closer to Him. We really wanted to please Him. Calvin made a commitment to God to stop cussing, stop fighting with me, and leaving totally the former lifestyle of womanizing behind, along with other issues we were having. We got married and had a very beautiful ceremony in the presence of God, friends and family. Even in that The Lord was smiling down on us. I only regret that all of my children did not see their father and I get married to each other. Two of our children were in our wedding, my young children were with my friend Dorene who was the girlfriend, at the time, of Calvin's nephew Tebo.

And after a very long time of fighting with each other, lots of sickness, good health, children, pain, tears, bad times and plenty of good times, we became one saved union under God. This, no doubt is the best decision that we could have ever made together and I thank God often for the love, togetherness, and peace that He has given us. The songs we chose at our wedding were truly fitting for our lives, Natalie Cole's "Our Love" and Etta James' "At Last". What a blessing it truly was, at last.

If you think about yesterday too long, you lose sight of your tomorrows

12

Toxic Friends and Aloneness

As a young adult, I had a core group of friends (or maybe I should say associates), at least five, and one was actually a best friend that was developed in high school and on through my first marriage. As the years passed, I'm not quite sure what happened but we all started drifting apart and sort of going our separate ways.

We could have been like sisters. Some of them did not know each other directly but I was friends with all of them. Martha Pierce was my best friend since my sophomore year of high school on through my first marriage and until Calvin and I met. I don't know why everyone always called her by her first and last name, it just seemed to fit. Valerie had been my best friend in grade school. Vickie was from freshman year of high school. I met Brenda through a mutual friend and Katy was a neighbor at my first apartment that me and my daughter moved into during my divorce. These are friends that I would go out to the club with, visit and talk on the phone with and just hang out. At least one of them was usually always available.

We all still were friends well after Calvin and I met, but not as close, then we started to drift away. I got back in touch with Martha Pierce on a fluke after being out of touch for probably twenty years. I just happened to be reading through the newspaper and saw there had been a death in her family. Then I ran into one of her cousins at the church that Calvin was performing at and gave her my number, asked to have Martha Pierce call me and she did. Boy was I shocked to hear from her. We stayed in contact for a while and she came out to my house to visit me. Little did I know, her brother Jarell would pass away around that same time. It was the early 2000's when he passed and after his funeral, during one of our conversations, I asked her if she knew that he and I had dated once and she said yes and told me how upset she was with both of us but couldn't or wouldn't say why. Who knew? Over the years, female associates have come and gone. I am not quite sure why my school friends and I did not stay friends but it was hurtful when we lost touch.

Nothing happened dramatically to cause us to drift apart over the years. We just simply got older, moved farther apart, priorities changed, and no one really put any effort in trying to keep our relationships going for years to come. I suppose that's just what happened, our values and priorities changed. As time goes on, it seems the value for friendships apparently became meaningless or perhaps selfish.

At any rate, I have learned how fickle and hurtful, we women can be to each other. We can stab and hurt for no solidly good reason, and not genuinely forgive someone when they say that they have forgiven. I feel that if you say something to me that offends me I should be able to let you know that you have just offended me, forgive you and we should be able to move on. If I offend you, you also should be able to forgive me and let us move forward. If you won't allow yourself to forgive, there is a horribly big flaw in your personality that you probably need to talk to God about to clean up in your life. Even if there is never an apology for the hurt, if we can't or won't let it go, God in heaven will not forgive us either.

Women tend to want to hold on to the pain, hurt and unforgiveness. It's been my experience that women can't or maybe won't take what they dish out. As I said before, that if I can accept you for who and what you are, why can't you accept me for who and what I am? We will not always agree, I may not always do what you think I should do or say what you want to hear, but does that mean we can't be friends anymore? And does it mean that I am written off now, for good? No doubt much prayer is needed in this case. And I still need to move on because forgiveness is for *me*. It has been a life long and complex lesson about my gender called "woman".

One thing that I would encourage anyone to do is to get away from, shake off, and let them go are those toxic friends. You know who they are. They are the people who claim to be your friends or at least act like they are your friends but do obvious things to let you know that they really don't mean you any good. For instance, a woman that always wants to be in your house but can never bring herself to give you a compliment. Or someone that only calls you when things are going rough for them and very seldom, if at all, inquire about how you are doing and if they can do anything for you instead of trying to get something from you. Or what about the friend who wants to pattern her life after yours in almost everything you do. I would call that jealousy, but it is a hidden jealousy, or so she thinks. If you're smart enough, you'll catch it. She is so jealous of you and your life that she wishes she could be you or wishes she could have what you have. And what about the person that never has a compliment for you but wants to always ask "is that new" or "did you get your hair done?" or "how much did that cost?" Instead of just saying, that looks good on you or you look nice today. These are the toxic people I'm talking about. Sadly enough, toxic people can even be in your own family. I have found that sometimes children grow up and can even be toxic to you. I prayed a prayer some years ago to the Lord that if I had to be around or be involved with women and people in general who do not mean me any good and who back bite, scandalize my name and just generally don't like me or hold unforgiveness in their heart, mind and spirit against me or hold anything negative against me, for Him to protect me from that, to let me be by myself with my husband. And you know God has kept me protected from that over the years. It has sometimes caused me to feel extremely alone and lonely. My telephone does not ring off the hook with family and friends inviting me here or there and I don't have a lot of friends that I can call to invite here or there. But one thing is for sure, God has surely protected me from the toxicidity of people that do not have my best interest at heart. There is a saying that goes, "friendship is not about how many people came and went, but it's about those who stayed."

A really true friend will not intentionally hurt you, desert you, or forsake you

13

The Transformation

I learned over time that God is a God of purpose. He has created us to fulfill a certain purpose in our lives. We are not just here to go to work, go to church, play and have fun. Nor are we here just to coexist, we are here to make a difference, to help each other with obstacles, trials and tribulations. We are also here to help, encourage, mend, train, teach, learn and love. There will always be hurting people in the world. Our duty, and most often it starts within our family, is to start somewhere with focusing on how we can help others. We're here to capture moments of time and to reflect on where we have come from so that we can keep focusing in on where we are going. So much precious time and so many wasted years have gone by where family is mad at each other, won't stay in touch and in some cases, care very little about each other. For what, to prove some pointless point. Family, and if we are fortunate enough to yield and keep one friend throughout life, is the most important thing we could ask for on earth. Our faith, family and friends are the keys to life on earth. These are keys that we should never lose. These are the elements that will help sustain us in our time of need and in some cases pain. These are also the elements that will hopefully be there when relationships fail, when alleged friends walk out of your life, when you lose a job, when the deal doesn't close, when the doctor says you need surgery or even when he says they've done all they can do for you. There is nothing greater on earth than to know that you have people praying for you, checking in on you and caring about you. To know that you don't have to go it alone. I cannot say this enough, please stop wasting time holding on to past hurt, anger and focusing on what and who has hurt you. I can almost assure you that *you* have hurt people in your life whether you know it or not. Everyone has. But forgiveness is a very, very powerful tool. If we can talk ourselves into staying upset with someone, we can talk ourselves into forgiving someone. Just let it go. Choose to not be a holding tank for garbage. God has given us all a free will. We are to exercise that free will, to fulfill His purpose in our lives *willingly*, and to make a difference with this life that He has given us. That is why He gives us children, to make a difference in their lives by nurturing, caring, instilling good and moral values in them, teaching them the right things to do and hope that they choose to do them and ultimately help them fulfill His purpose for their lives.

⚬⚭⚬

We had always taken our children trick or treating on Halloween, before we got reclaimed, to mostly neighborhoods and people that we knew. Calvin and I started watching a television program hosted by Herbert W Armstrong who was a Seventh Day Adventist Minister. Even though our faith was Baptist, we listened to many of the issues that Mr. Armstrong taught on. He taught on many different issues, most of which were from the Old Testament such as what to eat and what not to eat, the real meaning of Christmas and that it is a pagan holiday. He taught also about the devil's holiday, Halloween. We started realizing that a lot of what Mr. Armstrong was teaching all made sense.

We decided that we were not going to give up Christmas. We figured that if we explain to our children everything associated with Christmas, the Santa Claus, Christmas ornaments, and the Christmas tree, how none of it has anything to do with Jesus. We explained that Gold, Frankincense, the Three Wisemen, the Star that lead the Three Wisemen to Jesus, all of these things are directly related to Jesus, and that it would be ok and acceptable to God to give and exchange gifts. We also stressed to them that it is not how big a gift is but that it should come from one's heart. The devil's holiday is a bit different. This, we taught them, represented something evil. We started having them watch TBN around Halloween time with us and they would show different explanations on the origins of Halloween and about sacrificing, witches, and warlocks. We would explain the events and what was happening so that hey could understand it. Now, as they say, Rome was not built in a day. We found other entertainment for our children when Halloween came around. The church we were attending had a carnival, with a movie, games and candy giveaway. The kids really liked that. We also used to play games at home and I'd make caramel corn, popcorn, and buy lots of candy, apples and all kinds of stuff for them. I really believe they didn't mind not going out trick-or-treating anymore. My youngest child was born into our family not really experiencing trick-or-treating and didn't experience it until he was around thirteen years old and that was because one of his siblings influenced him to go. I understand now that not only was Calvin and I being transformed but we were in the process of transforming our children as well. We learned that if you're trying to change things in your life, you just have to start right where you're at, no putting it off, just do it.

If life is but a vapor then breathe in and breathe in deeply

14

Children and Abuse by Disregard

YOUNG, vibrant and full of life, but no nonsense when it came to disciplining kids. That was me. It also became a custom to mix a grownup party with the kids' party. In fact, because Little Lonnie was born on my birthday, he grew up with us having birthday celebrations together. It was a family tradition until he moved to San Diego in 2003 and even now, we still always connect on our birthday, whether by phone or in person, it's our day.

The children always had all types of friends from different and diverse cultures over, from Asian to Black to Indian to White to Mexican to African, just to name a few. I believe I was pretty successful with encouraging my children to not be prejudiced against people because of their color or national origin. They were raised to be comfortable in their own skin and to be cool with whoever treated them ok. To not put all people into one big fat group and say "I'm not going to like them because they are white" or whatever the case might be. It was always refreshing to see whenever we had birthday parties or some kind of function at our house that the kids' friends always felt comfortable coming to our functions and just coming to the house to hang out with our kids. Our home, in a sense was like the United Nations, different personalities, ethnicities and cultures. There was a time when I even gave several of their friends some motherly advice on more than one occasion. Calvin loaned one of the guys a jacket and tie to make sure that he looked very nice for his senior prom.

All of the friends of our children loved and respected us and that always made me feel good as a mother and as a person. But even so, it's very difficult to raise children. As every parent knows, there is no handbook or guidelines that come with children. No one has it perfectly right. Sometimes children that are successful might think that they are successful because of their own merit, or because they worked so hard and struggled so much and overcame obstacles that were put in their way, and some did but *they didn't go it alone.* Whether our children ever admit it or not, my parenting abilities coupled with my husband's stern ability has helped to encourage them, has been a shoulder for them to lean on when needed, has helped them to see life a little clearer, and set them on the right path. I've personally had the honor of opening their eyes to the business and corporate world, and tried to instill the importance of good work ethics in them. It was a purpose of mine to always make myself available for them, and helped them see themselves as successful, to nudge them out into the real working world and called them out and chastised them when they needed it.

For all of you who are or are not parents that have done that, my hat is off to you. I understand your plight. It has been my experience that no matter how lenient you are or how mean and strict you are, the children are either going to love you unconditionally or they won't. They will either forgive your shortcomings or they won't. They will accept you for who you are, or they won't. And for those that don't, they need to step back and really, really think about it. I'm not saying I was not hard on the kids because we had to be tough on the kids that we raised. Some of Mother's ways may have rubbed off on to me in that I never could stand for any child to sass back or when I tell them to go do something they don't move until they get ready. I expected better than that. But no matter how I felt about them as a person, it never stopped me from helping them out even when they acted ugly toward me. Sometimes children seem to think that they are all that. That they *never* give you a reason to *not* like them. And that whatever they say or do, no way could they ever be lying or stretching the truth...just a little. Even if I did not always like them, I always loved them. But as time goes on and the children grow up, unless they are just plain evil, (and perhaps some are) time heals all wounds.

There comes a time in people's lives when you are not a child anymore and you should realize it's time to start acting like an adult and put away childish things. It probably never occurred to them that they did not make it easy for me to always *like* them but that I did always love them. Although it very rarely happens, it is quite nice to receive a word of encouragement from some of the children occasionally. It is equally nice when they do something special for me and Calvin. Most of our children do great things for both of us from their heart because they love us *equally*.

One of the children, Yazzmin, who has children now and has gone through some life events of her own, has given me some encouragement in knowing just through general conversation, that she now understands my position as one who has not been fully accepted or respected by some members of our family. She further understands that when someone is different, that sometimes we are set apart and perhaps even envied by not just some within the family but by people in general. Yazzmin has had to deal with this very thing herself. It is not comforting for me to realize that for her to fully understand what has been happening to me all these years, that it is now happening to her. She knows that I love her as I do all the children but there is something about talking it out, there's something supernatural about sharing your feelings and trusting each other while sharing your feelings. There's also healing in sharing and talking. I could feel burdens being lifted off my shoulders when we had our talk, especially when she told me she now understands my position. No one has ever come to me and said anything like that before. To take ownership of what you have done (or not done) to someone and to voice it to the person is just a tremendous thing to do. Not very many people have that kind of love for another person. Not very many people would be willing to lay their pride down and show their true selves like that. And not too many people are even willing to try to begin to see and understand your plight or give you *some* benefit of the doubt and say 'maybe I could have tried to be a little more understanding' or 'could have been a little more cooperative.'

It has been a lot of years of a painful struggle with some of the children to find love in their hearts for me as a parent. I can only hope the day will come when they will stop disregarding me by separating Calvin and me with their actions. This is what I call silent abuse or abuse by disregard. God feels my tears and hears my prayers. I pray for the day when the walls will come down and our entire blended family will truly love one another and realize that forgiveness is not for the weak, it is for the strong. True forgiveness is a sure sign of hope, love and maturity on all levels.

Try putting action to the words "I love you"

15

The Vicious Cycle - Relational Dysfunction

I used to worry about the fact that me and my own daughter are not close. I have done a lot of soul searching on this one and realized early in my adult life that Mother had the bond with Julisa. It's like a vicious cycle or a nightmare that I can't wake up from. At the time she was born I was very young, still living at home and had one more year of high school left. I knew nothing about babies; had never even babysat anyone else's kid let alone raise one of my own.

This baby girl of mine, grew up resenting me as her mother because I was the enforcer of rules and regulations, the "bad guy" so to speak and Mother was the spoiler or the "good guy." So needless to say there was always constant battling and temper tantrums from Julisa when I would tell her to do something and Mother would step in because she believed in letting her have her way. Mother had totally flip flopped from the way she had been with me. She now was an old person trying to make things right with God through my daughter, creating a monster in the process. When Julisa was about two during the time I filed for divorce from her father James, we moved into an apartment. I got a job at a nursing care facility and Julisa, needless to say, was spending even more time with Mother. Mother had kept her everyday while I finished my last year of high school, she would keep her if I went out, and she kept her really whenever I needed her to. Realizing late in life I was creating a relational dysfunction. I am not in denial about anything. Mother had control over my daughter. If it were possible, that part of my life I would change. So this little girl grew up being chastised by me and spoiled by Mother quite frequently.

After we moved into the apartment, my daughter loved staying with Mother and learned very young in life that she was her spoiler. She knew that all she had to do was throw a tantrum, fall out and scream and Mother to the rescue. Most of the time I gave in and let Julisa go ahead and spend the night with her and whenever I gave in, Julisa would immediately be all right. This went on for years. No matter how much I talked to Julisa, or spanked her when she'd act like that, the worse she got. I loved my daughter very much but she proved to be more challenging for me than all three of my sons put together. One thing is for sure, no lie can live forever.

Things came to a head after several years of ups, downs and emotional roller coaster rides. I had quit smoking after seventeen years, my last baby had been born, Calvin and I had gotten married after an extremely long waiting period. Nothing tremendously outlandish was going to happen right? Everything was going so wonderfully, right? Wrong, not too long after we got married, I had left one morning to go to the beauty shop. Little Lonnie had been grounded a few days before so he was to stay inside while his brother Jarmane got to go out and play. When I got back from the beauty shop that afternoon, my daughter now almost sixteen years old, and Calvin had this big blow up about her wanting to go somewhere probably to the mall and not doing what I told her to do which was to add something to the household savings. Julisa had a part time job at the time. One of the rules of the house for the children was that if you have a job, and living at home you are to contribute something to the household.

That has always been the standard rule for all of the kids that lived at home. I'm not saying they liked it, or agreed with it, but that was the rule. The purpose of this was to teach them responsibility while they are young and the meaning of what it takes to run a house while actually helping out the household to benefit everyone in the house. Calvin and I are from the Old School and this was the rule at home for me and Calvin except our amounts were higher than what we had set for our kids. I also could not have a key to the house plus only a minimal amount of company. She was always one that never liked the rules of the house, chores and could stand right in your face and lie. Calvin reiterated to her, that before she leaves to go anywhere that she is to contribute her amount to the house that we had set and to do her chores. She resisted and told him in no uncertain terms that she was not going to do that and that she did not see any reason for it and how unfair it was. So he told her, "ok, since you don't want to mind, put on your old clothes to go to the mall and not wear those brand new clothes that you just bought".

According to Calvin's account she turned into another person or I should say "another thing" something demonic. He said she yelled out at him, loud enough for all of the kids and neighbors around outside to hear, "I'm not taking off sh_t!" I thank God that Little Lonnie *was* grounded that day. We lived in a townhouse so Lonnie, Julisa and Calvin were all upstairs. Jarmane was in and out of the house all that day and Lonnie was in his room playing and talking out the window to his brother and the other neighborhood kids. So thank God he heard and seen everything. Calvin said that Julisa then went into the bathroom (he and she had originally been just in the upstairs hallway.) She dropped on the closed toilet seat saying, "oh my God, I can't believe I just said that". Calvin said he then just turned and walked away from her leaving her talking to herself in disbelief at what she had just done and telling her he was going to whip her. That was the fatal blow that drove the final nail into the coffin for my daughter and me. Julisa and I already had a very shaky relationship and this just finished it off. Now I was put in a very precarious predicament, to choose my husband or my daughter, which is exactly where Julisa wanted me to be. Calvin was in a very awkward position as well.

When I came home from the beauty salon, my husband told me what happened and my daughter told me what happened. The two versions were not the same, they were very different. Julisa's version was that Calvin tried to touch her and make her have sex with him. She was crying, and acting very upset. I was in disbelief but not totally shocked because I knew everyone under my roof all too well from the youngest to the oldest. After talking to my daughter, checking out her demeanor, her answers and being molested so many times as a child myself, I knew the signs. She was lying. I then did the obvious, I questioned her ten year old brother Little Lonnie about what he had seen and heard. He told me pretty much the same thing Calvin had told me and how "Julisa cussed at Daddy," was his words. He was just as flabbergasted as I was and probably a little scared for his sister at what he thought I would do to her since Calvin chose to not punish her. *He never once said or implied that Calvin touched her inappropriately in any way at all.* I don't really remember how the rest of the evening went but one thing I did have to do was asked my husband if what my daughter had told me was true. As a mother, a human being and a woman, that question had to be asked, knowing full well that was totally out of character for him. Calvin assured me that no way would he ever touch her or anyone else's daughter for that matter. He understood why he had to be questioned by me. Calvin has four girls of his own and was and is very protective of them. I already knew, in my gut and in my soul that he would not do anything to hurt her, himself or me.

Forgive, even if you've never gotten an apology from one who has lied on you, or caused pain and grief in your life

16

The Final Cut

THE decision I made to not wreck my marriage and leave Calvin would finish off the already messed up mother/daughter relationship between Julisa and I. Two days later after Julisa wasn't sure if Calvin was going to whip her or not since he kept assuring her that he was, Little Lonnie gave me a note that his sister had given to him and told him to give it to me. In the note she had written that she was in the obvious place and that Calvin had made her do things that she did not want to do on several different occasions. My daughter had run away to Mother's house and her story had changed already and kept changing over the years.

One of the versions was that I even held her down while Calvin molested her. I called Mother and advised her to send her back home. Of course Mother was not going to do that. She wanted her there with her. I talked to Julisa and told her that I would ask her only once to come back home, so I did and she did not come home. I told her she would need to report the assault to the police, and be checked out by a doctor, she refused on all accounts. She definitely did not want the police involved because she knew they were trained to dig and get at the truth which would have exposed her as being a liar. Julisa was with me in the hospital (before this all happened) when Deon was born in June and was gone by her 17th birthday that next year. So for the next twenty one years, and perhaps forever, Julisa would stay stopped in time. My decision to believe my husband over my daughter would prove to haunt me from that time until now. She tried to create a wedge between our family, our friends and us. Not only did the family know of the lie that Julisa had created against her stepfather and me, but she was also telling and trying to convince our friends to believe this horrific story of hers. Anyone she'd meet that she thought would be interested in her story, she told it to.

I realize why she had to continue on with her charade of lies for the rest of her life. First, she wanted freedom from rules and regulations of the house and to be able to come and go as she pleased, she could not do that at home, only at Mother's house. Secondly, because after lying all those months and then suddenly come clean with the truth, she would have exposed *herself* as being a liar. Thirdly, it would make her look extremely bad as a person and to the world to admit that she had been lying all this time bringing about shame and embarrassment to herself. I have heard and read about women who had left their husbands and boyfriends just to find out that the girl had lied on him and the woman realized that she had made a horrific mistake. The driving factor for me was simple. Being an abuse survivor myself and being very much in tune with my children, I knew what to look for. *Calvin had no sexually abusive motives or traits in his mind, body or soul.* He had helped me raise Julisa from the time she was three years old. He treated her like a daughter. During the time before all this happened Julisa and Calvin got along well except when Mother would try to turn her against him by making wise crack remarks about him.

When Julisa got older and started getting interested in learning how to drive a car he even took her driving once and she almost ran into the fence in the apartment units that we lived in but he got the car stopped in time, thank goodness. On a couple of occasions she asked him if she could go to the dog races with him, at first he said no but then changed his mind once and told her she could go because he felt empathy for her do to her own father not being in her life. There she did happen to run into her father and tried to talk to him but he, I was told by Julisa and Calvin, didn't really have time or take time to talk to her like he should have.

That was, for the most part, Jimmy's way, never had time. He was not consistent in her life at all. I can't help but think that those times she would keep asking Calvin if she could go to the track with him or take her driving, that she was plotting to try and destroy both of our characters then.

As the years went by Julisa and I went on what I like to call, a roller coaster ride. Sometimes we'd be ok and could talk, laugh and have fun over the telephone and if I said anything in any way to contradict her or not agree with her about something, the abuse would come. I was called a bit_h several times over the phone then she'd just slam the phone down in my face.

More years went by, Mother was now old and becoming very forgetful, later she would be diagnosed with dementia but she was still living in her own home and allowing Julisa to live there whenever she and her fiancé DeRon wanted to. In 1998 after finding out that Julisa was taking advantage of Mother by writing large checks against her checking account for alleged medications for her baby, I confronted her about it one Sunday afternoon. Calvin and Mother was in the living room, Julisa and I were in the kitchen along with her two daughters and DeRon was staying out of sight in the basement. All I asked her was why was she taking advantage of an old person by taking her money and why didn't she as a mother have a place of her own to live for her little family. She started spewing things out of her mouth that no one, let alone a daughter should ever let come out of their mouth to their mother or any one else for that matter.

The last thing I remember her saying before I fired on her repeatedly was her standing toe to toe in my face telling me fu _ k him and fu _k you too! I must have blacked out because I don't remember seeing or hearing DeRon come up from the basement but I do remember my hands were not moving anymore, for some reason. It felt like something strong had caused them to resist. DeRon had grabbed both of hands pulling me away from Julisa. Calvin had grabbed DeRon scuffling with him and telling him "let her go man!" When I came to myself and my head finally stopped spinning, Julisa was on the floor crying telling me she was not going to fight me, her girls were crying at the kitchen table, Mother was crying and upset and after Calvin got DeRon away from me DeRon was telling us that we've got to get out of here. Imagine that, this is Mother's house but he's trying to put *us* out. Julisa then started yelling and saying, "you've fuc_ed up now bit_ h!" I did not know that it was a felony to hit someone in the presence of minor children. She on the other hand knew it.

Later after we got home, Calvin called the children that had already moved away from home and asked them to come over and join the rest of the kids as moral support for me, he knew that Julisa had called the police. Later that night, around 1am, the police would come to arrest me but didn't. It was the grace of God again that brought me through that whole ordeal. My record, character and credibility was excellent, but my daughter's was not. After questioning me, and hearing my side of what happened, the arresting officer gave me her card and suggested that *I* get a restraining order against Julisa. We did that the very next day and even ran into Julisa and DeRon in the courthouse.

This was such a trying and regretful time in my life. The bottom line is, some time had passed and I didn't know that my daughter had pressed charges and there was a warrant for my arrest. The warrant happened to come in the mail the day before Calvin and I were to leave on our road trip to Alabama on the bus. Oh my goodness, first we called the courthouse they told us I had to post bail, and have a hearing before a judge to get the ok to even leave the state. They told us that I could not go and post my own bail or else I would be arrested right on the spot because of the warrant. It was crazy. I had no idea any of this was going on behind the scenes. Technically, the police could have come to my job or my home and taken me away in handcuffs, at any time.

We had to go into our vacation money so that Calvin could go to the justice center after the hearing and post my bail. We did make our road trip but court hearings were still looming over my head. Julisa kept having the case set over. So after about a year and a half, I had to go to court for something like a domestic violence hearing and the judge finally threw the case out with only stating to me to keep my hands to myself, and I agreed. I'm sure Julisa did not want to continue the hearings or press charges any further for fear that her, let's just say, "colorful life" would have been exposed. And, by God's mercy and grace, my record had spoke for itself. I'm not proud that I let my temper get the best of me that day but like I said before, everything happens for a reason and this would be the defining factor for the end of Julisa abusing her grandmother financially and verbally.

Mother trusted me and knew that Calvin and I would always try to do the right thing towards her, even though I had a very abusive and hurtful childhood, I still would do the right thing towards her.

As for my two granddaughters, Julisa has held on to the molestation lie and taught it to them, so needless to say she has kept them from having any sort of relationship with me. I'm sure the assault they witnessed in Mother's kitchen that day did not help. But I still classify this as lifelong relational abuse and dysfunction. At the time of this writing my granddaughters are eleven and almost seventeen years old. They know who I am but we are strangers, thanks to their mother lying, keeping them from me, and turning them against me early on. One day they will learn and accept the truth.

One needs to realize where they have been to visualize where they are going

17

Mother's Day, 2003

THIS day, May 11, was going to be just like any other Mother's Day, I thought. We all would go to church, my husband would take me out to dinner. The kids that lived at home would probably go out with us to eat. The one's that were out on their own would come by with cards and gifts. Our grandson Jerrel, along with his mother Elaine, would bring me flowers. That was not the case. It was a cool, bright and sunny day. I woke up extra early to get ready for church. Something told me to get my shower and prepare my clothes the night before so that we could hopefully get to church on time for Mother's Day service.

Soon after I got into my bright orange skirt and jacket the telephone rang about 8:30 that Sunday morning. It was Miss Lillian, the Adult Foster Care nurse who had been taking care of Mother ever since she had come from the hospital in November. She was letting me know that Mother had taken ill suddenly and the ambulance was taking her to the hospital right away. I remember my heart racing and anxiety started setting in. Something was seriously wrong because she never calls unless there is a problem. She sounded a little panicked as I recall, as she was telling me that Mother was fine previously. Miss Lillian said twice that she just didn't know what happened because there was no sign that anything was wrong. I told her it would take me a few minutes to get to the hospital since I lived a little ways from it but I was taking off immediately. I called Julisa to let her know that her Grandmother was being taken to the hospital and her condition sounded dire. She said she was leaving shortly to go to the hospital. When I got there I let the nurses and emergency room doctors know who I was and asked to see Mother. They said it would be a few minutes before I could see her. After about a half an hour Julisa showed up. I let her know what they had told me.

They finally let us in to see Mother. We did not get there in enough time to say our last goodbyes. Her breathing was shallow, her tongue was thick and clung to the roof of her mouth. Mother's eyes were closed. I knew that she would take her last breath any minute now. By now Julisa and I were holding hands like two little lost children and Julisa was audibly crying. The tears streamed down my face but silently. I held one of Mother's hands as she breathed a few more shallow breaths then finally the shallow breathing stopped.

One of the nurses was standing there with Julisa and I. Even after Mother had stopped breathing it seemed like she had just fallen asleep. Shock may have set in on me briefly because I told the nurse she seems like she's gone to sleep. Going back to the time of working in a nursing home facility, it had been about eighteen years since I had actually touched someone who had just expired. I had forgotten the eerie and overwhelming feeling of disconnect and loss. This was different for me. It was Mother. It seemed like she should have been here forever. I could not believe that I had just witnessed her leaving this world, at this time.

As I recall, the nurse felt for her pulse then said yes she's gone. I was still holding her hand and just whispered, now she's in Jesus' arms. Julisa seemed to let go of her hand kind of abruptly when she realized that Mother had died. I know it can be traumatizing for some people to even be around the dead. After standing there quite a few minutes with Mother when she expired, the doctor told me that she had previously been laughing and talking to them, but that she had ultimately taken this turn. He said that she was peaceful just before her passing and that it would have been even more traumatizing physically on her if they had tried to resuscitate her. Well I know for a fact that is true from my years of working in a nursing home environment.

Mother and I had had several conversations in the past about life support machines and resuscitation. Her statement was, "when God close these eyes just let me go on home. I don't want no life support." She had filled out an advance directive and knew full well what she did and did not want. It was my job to pass the information on and see to it that her wishes were carried out. I called Calvin while at the hospital and called him again on the way home. He always knows just what to say to try to make me feel better. He advised me to be very careful and cautious driving home. I knew where he was coming from, my Mother had just passed away and I was with her when it happened, quietly distraught and in tremendous shock. He knew I must have felt numb and somewhat like a zombie on that freeway.

Upon arriving home, my husband and the two youngest children who were still living at home all greeted me at the door and wrapped their arms around me, that's when it finally hit me that my mother, who raised me, who beat me unmercifully, who knew how to torture but did not know how to truly love, had just passed away. I finally let loose and cried and cried. Afterward, I said to them I still want to go to church, and we did. So Mother's Day 2003 was a little different that year. The meaning went to a whole different level and it was undeniably an unforgettable one for me.

Let your healing begin with love

18

Ministry - God's Final Call

As a child, I used to see people getting saved and falling out under the power of the Holy Spirit, but it was always so frightening to me. It was fun going to Sunday school but when that afternoon service started and pastor Daniels would start preaching in "high gear" he would go through the church laying hands on and just set fire to the whole place! The church was a small but very effective Pentecostal congregation. It had probably about three hundred members starting out, maybe more. But it was a close knit body. People traveled a very long distance to get there sometimes. I suppressed getting filled with the Holy Ghost until I became an adult. Even then I was a little apprehensive. So this fear factor had over shadowed me getting Holy Ghost filled early. My love for God and the church was never shattered, no matter what my circumstances were, no matter what happened in my life, I was taught and always knew in my heart that God loved me. Mother used to say that "everything happens for a reason," I always believed that. It wasn't until all four of my children were born, two miscarriages, a nervous breakdown, a very long and sometimes turbulent relationship with Calvin, a messy first marriage, ongoing conflict with baby momma drama, always kids around and not to mention an ongoing never ending battle of an ugly temperament about my biological mother inside of me that just would not go away, that God was calling me. He has given me an assignment, a commission.

I began to realize that He had allowed me to go through drama, trauma, and tribulation "for a reason." It was beginning to become a little clearer why. I was learning that He often will allow you to go through things, fix you up and then put you right back in that same arena or want you to use that as a guideline for what ever it is He has for you to do. If you have never experienced anything, how can you inform, educate, enlighten or empower others? If you haven't gone through the stuff, then how can you truly say "I know how you feel?" or "I know what you're going through?" This is why I do not believe whole heartedly in therapists. Someone that has only "book learning" cannot always listen objectively and offer advice if they have not been where you are. I feel if you've never walked in my shoes, then you can't speak on my issues. You *don't* know how I feel about this. You can't possibly "understand my frustration." I do believe everyone has a story to tell or has gone through something but not everyone can or will talk about what they have experienced and most times that is the best teacher of all. Experience can also promote your own healing. That is my calling, to encourage those who have been badly discouraged, to offer some kind of glimpse of hope that if God brought me through all of this junk, He can and will bring you through too. To look at my own situation and realize that God has brought me through, time and time again and He won't let me down now. To know where to direct someone when I don't have the answer to their complex question. To not write people off even when they have written me off. Even though some have tried and succeeded to have slandered and dragged my name through the ground and accused falsely, to still be able to hold my head high. To not hold unforgiveness in my heart, as others' hold it against me. To be a living testimony is ultimately a gift from The Lord, and the story should be told.

I agree totally with Bishop Jakes when he says, "I want to talk to someone who has been through some stuff! If you've never been through anything, then you can't talk to me."

In conclusion, through it all after being dragged through all the muck and garbage, by men, women and yes even some children, I have decided to put it all into perspective by realizing it takes a very different kind of woman to befriend me and not write me off, I realize what kind that is. It takes a different kind of man to love me, I know what kind that is. It takes a different kind of child to put aside those punishments, scoldings and times of unfairness that I may have done, I know what kind that is. All of these have one quality in common and it is the *true* love of God in their heart powered by the Holy Spirit. These people are not being driven by their own prejudices, dislikes, unforgiveness, and disregard but driven by the Holy Spirit. How can you say you love God and yet you show very little regard for me? It hurts some to even ask how I'm doing but think they are doing a great work when they do a good deed for a stranger. And how do "church people" think they are going to get into heaven when they too have very little regard for each other? I have actually experienced being snubbed and disregarded while being involved in events and ministry within the church building. But nevertheless, God is shaking up some things, waking up some things, separating some things and restoring some things. He is nudging on those who will heed His call because one day, this life will be over and God will play back our lives and all will give an account of why they did what they did whether good or bad before and after they proclaimed salvation.

One thing is for sure that when it's all over, all will spend the rest of eternity in one place or the other.

If you don't like your present situation, let it be a motivator and don't complain too much, you just may get what you asked for

The Last Word

What's love got to do with it? *Everything*

As I have said before, love and forgiveness are the keys that are the determining factors in how you treat yourself, your family and your friends. It will also determine how we treat a stranger. Ask yourself some questions. Do I really treat others the way *I* want to be treated? Do I really, earnestly care about them? For those of us in the house of faith, the Christians, how can we sit in church with a clear conscious, praising God, some dancing in the spirit, go through all the motions and still act like a devil to members of our own families, not to mention fellow Christians. One of the main messages of Jesus was love.

Family has always been very important to me and as long as there is breath in my body, family will always be important. It is scriptural that children have a responsibility to honor their parents. Honor means to regard highly, an exalted title or rank. A child who honors their parent is adding life to themselves. I know for a fact that my husband and I honored both of our parents until their deaths. The roles had somewhat reversed. Our parents were old and needed our care.

My mother-in-law lived with my sister-in-law and she would come to our house to spend a few days at a time. Calvin was a good son to his mother, and she really showed that she loved her youngest son. He always made sure that he treated her with the utmost respect, and always carried out what she would ask of him until her death in 2008. With me and Mother, even though she treated me so unkindly and cruel growing up, it did not make me bitter towards her. It is true that going to her house was not high on my list; probably everyone knows that Mother was negative and was still somewhat mean even in her old age. But she developed dementia and became childlike, dependant.

Even though so many negative events were always thrust upon me, I was quick tempered but also quick to forgive, I'm thankful that God has given me a spirit of forgiveness. He knew that I wanted the finer things of life with Mother. He knew that I wanted a mother that would go to the movies with me, have coffee with, and have girl time with. He also knew that that would never be and that my role on this earth was not to be friends with Mother but it all was a test of my heart and a test to see if I would ignore the Holy Ghost and hold anger, hurt, unforgiveness and all that ugliness in my heart against her for the rest of *her* life. Would I get satisfaction out of seeing *her* now in need of physical care and start abusing her, would I allow my own daughter to abuse her, would I let her be hurt in any way, would I throw her away into a nursing home in sometimes awful conditions that are not even fit, in some cases, for dogs to live in? Absolutely not. Did what I endured make me or break me? I say it made me. It made me strong in my faith in God. It made me realize that no matter what you think life should be, God has something He wants to accomplish in *you* and He has a purpose for your life. My time in this world has often been a rough one, a not so easy one and a not so fair one. Bearing children, not so easy, raising children, not so easy, working hard all my life, not so easy. Marriage, not so easy, swallowing my pride many times, not easy at all, biting my tongue, not so easy. Even forgiving, not always quite so easy. But I decided not to let unforgiveness stay in my spirit, rooting up the seeds of bitterness and ultimately, one day keeping my soul from entering the pearly gates of heaven. Jesus said, that if we want forgiveness, then we must ourselves forgive. What has been easy is praising and thanking God for this journey that He has set me on through life and using me to be a testimony of His goodness and mercy. My relationship with Him does not cost anything. It has already been bought and paid for in blood with no gimmicks, no false promises just true unconditional love and blessings from on high.

The past can and has been forgiven and maybe one day, forgotten. No one cried for me but I cried plenty for myself and thank God I do not have to cry anymore.

Some food for thought, choose to not hold unforgiveness against anyone, because in doing so, you are releasing healing for yourself and not letting satan win. Try to make it a habit to encourage or compliment someone else frequently, from your heart, for by doing so you are building that person up from the inside out. You never know who needs an encouraging word from you. Follow your dreams; do not be deterred by listening too much to the opinions of everyone else. Encourage yourself, others won't give you that often enough, so don't look for it. Make it a practice to forgive often; it keeps your soul clear. Lastly, say what is meaningful while you yet can, because words and deeds will not matter when time has finally run out.

Encouragement does not cost you anything but it can mean everything to someone else.

Sherree

Dedicated to all those who have been abused, rejected, hurt and slandered, you do matter.